CONTENTS

ISBN 978-90-823048-5-5
First Edition – April 2015

© Haakpret Veghel
Illustrations, Design, Instructions: Anja Toonen
Author: Anja Toonen
English Translation: Linda Tsardakas

Preface

What could be nicer than to reproduce an idea, to make a small something by hand to give as a gift to a good friend or someone you love? This booklet is full of ideas for you to crochet or to inspire you to create your own designs. An item crocheted by hand is unique and therefore very special. Have fun crocheting!

Anja Toonen

Materials

Yarn for the fat fabulous ladies and the gentleman:
I used Scheepjeswol Larra (50 g / 125 m, cotton) for all models, crocheted with a 2.5 mm crochet hook.
Sitting ladies: 19 cm / 7½ ins high; standing ladies: 22 cm / 8¾ ins high.
If you use a more heavyweight or lightweight yarn, or a different size crochet hook, or work more loosely or tightly, your figures will be smaller or larger in size.

Yarn for the hair of the fat fabulous ladies:
A different yarn is used for each lady. Basically, any yarn is suitable. I like to use Firenze by Scheepjeswol because it is nice and curly. You may also use Larra by Scheepjeswol. The basic instructions explain the different hair styles.
I also prefer flat crochet hooks because the hook then automatically points in the right direction. I also find flat hooks require less effort to work with.

Florist's wire, side cutters, and flat nose or needle nose pliers:
I used florist's wire (about 1.4 cm/ a good ½ in thick) to allow the ladies out for a walk and the dancing couple to stand. The wire must be supple but yet firm enough to give the legs stability. I also used florist's wire for the dog's legs, the dancers' arms and for the cocktail.
As an alternative for the sunglasses for the lady at the beach, you can use a paper clip instead of florist's wire.

Filling: I recommend using washable filling (available at hobby shops or at department stores). If you tend to crochet loosely, first insert a nylon stocking into the figure or object and then place the filling in it.

Yarn Requirements

The requirements listed are just a guideline. The exact amount will depend on your personal crochet (if you work loose or tight stitches) and on the size of your crochet hook.

Fat Fabulous Ladies:

Scheepjeswol Larra (50 g / 125 m, cotton), crocheted with a 2.5 mm crochet hook:
1 ball of each colour, light flesh colour number 7355.
Hair: 1 ball Firenze curly yarn in rust brown colour number 12 or black colour number 11.
Scheepjeswol Sicilia in rust brown colour number 13 (gentleman), black colour number 11.

Armchair and Sofa:

Scheepjeswol Larra (50 g / 125 m, cotton), crocheted with a 2.5 mm crochet hook:
Sofa: 3 balls in the main colour, light grey colour number 7407.
Armchair: 2 balls in the main colour, dark grey colour number 7406.
Cushions: white colour number 7310, 1 ball is enough for 5 cushions.

Air Mattress and Air Mattress Chair:

Scheepjeswol Larra (50 g / 125 m, cotton), crocheted with a 2.5 mm crochet hook:
1 ball in each colour is enough for both items.
1 ball in brown colour number 7419 for the back and the sides.

General Tips

<u>To decrease 1 double crochet</u> (= dec 1): Always insert hook just into the front loop of the stitch. This will make the decrease less visible. Work the dec 1 = decrease 1 double crochet as follows: Insert crochet hook into ftl of both following sts, yarn over hook and pull thread through, then yarn over hook and pull thread through all loops on hook (also see illus. below right).

<u>To crochet off:</u> Leave a length of thread hanging at the end of the last round and pass through the last stitch. Use this thread later to sew the pieces together and then conceal the remainder of the thread.

<u>There are three methods of ending a round;</u>
- close a round with a sl st, begin the next rnd with 1 ch;
- turn the work at the end of a round and work back in the other direction;
- use a contrasting thread to mark the beginning of the round and continue in spiral rounds.
Note: The number of rounds depends on the method used to end a round. Therefore, always follow the instructions as given. The shape of the design is based on a good count during the round. therefore alsways follow the instructions as given.

Important rule: A sl st worked into a round is counted as a stitch – just the same as the other stitches. There is one exception to this rule: Do not count the st st if it is used to close a rnd.

<u>Crochet off 2 tr together:</u> Work 1 tr each into the following sts as follows: * 1 yarn over, insert hook into following st, 1 yarn over and pull thread through, with 1 yarn over pull thread through 2 loops on the hook, rep from * 1x, then 1 yarn over and pull thread through all loops on the hook.

Basic Crochet Techniques

Basic crochet techniques can be found on my website.
You can also download the illustrated workshops as a PDF file.
In dutch or german language only.
Dutch: www.haakpret.nl - button Download and picture 'basistechnieken'.
German: www.haekelfreude.de - button Download 'grundtechniken' and picture 'basistechnieken'.

Abbreviations (British Crochet Terms)

ch	= chain stitch(es)	dtr	= double treble crochet (double trebles)
sl st	= slip stitch(es)	[ ]	= total number of stitches on a row/rnd
dc	= double crochet	row	= row
inc 1	= increase one double crochet (work 2 dc into the same point of insertion)	rnd	= round
		bkl	= back loop of stitch
dec 1	= decrease 1 dc (see page 2)	ftl	= front loop of stitch
tr	= treble crochet	beg	= begin
		rep	= repeat
htr	= half treble crochet (half trebles)	CT	= contrasting thread

Begin with a thread ring as illustrated.
You can also download the PDF illustrating the basic techniques from my website.

Mark start of rnd with a contrasting thread (= CT), continue in spiral rounds: Lay the contrasting thread between the last double crochet stitch and the first double crochet stitch of the next round; always pass the CT to the next round as you work.

  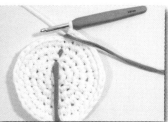

Decrease 1 double crochet: Insert the crochet hook into the *ftl* of both following stitches (left illus.), lay yarn over hook and pull yarn through (centre illus.), then yarn over hook and pull through all loops on hook (right illus.)

Changing colours: End the rnd before with a sl st; work the 1st ch in the new colour (see illus. left and centre). Illustration below right: Work double crochet into the back loop of the stitch.

BASIC INSTRUCTIONS FAT FABULOUS LADIES

BASIC INSTRUCTIONS:

All fat fabulous ladies are crocheted according to the following basic instructions.
Any differences are mentioned in the specific instructions for each model.

Head: Flesh colour
1: 6 dc into a thread ring, close with 1 sl st.
2: 1 ch, 1 dc, 2x (3 dc in 1 st), 1 dc, 2x (3 dc in 1 st) [14 sts], place CT marker, continue in spiral rnds.
3: 3 dc, 3x inc 1, 4 dc, 3x inc 1, 1 dc [20 sts].
4: 1 dc, inc 1, 3 dc, inc 1, 1 dc, inc 1, 3 dc, inc 1, 3 dc, inc 1, 1 dc, inc 1, 2 dc [26 sts].
5: 3x (inc 1, 3 dc), 1 dc, inc 1, 4 dc, 2x (inc 1, 3 dc) [32 sts].
6: 2 dc, inc 1, 5 dc, inc 1, 8 dc, inc 1, 8 dc, inc 1, 5 dc [36 sts].
7: 16 dc, inc 1, 8 dc, inc 1, 10 dc [38 sts].
8 to 10: 38 dc.
11: 17 dc, 6x dec 1, 9 dc [32 sts].
12: 3 dc, dec 1, 12 dc, work into ftl; 6x inc 1, work into both loops of stitch from here;

9 dc [37 sts].
13: 13 dc, dec 1, 14 dc, dec 1, 6 dc [35 sts].
14: 11 dc, dec 1, 16 dc, dec 1, 4 dc [33 sts].
15: dec 1, 3 dc, dec 1, 2 dc, dec 1, 18 dc, dec 1, 2 dc [29 sts].
From here work all dc into bkl (the hair will later be worked into ftl)
16: 10 dc, dec 1, 12 dc, dec 1, 3 dc [27 sts].
17: 3x (7 dc, dec 1) [24 sts].
18: 6x (2 dc, dec 1) [18 sts].
19: 6x (1 dc, dec 1) [12 sts], insert filling into head
20: 4x 3 dc crocheted off together [4 sts].
Crochet off all sts, pass thread through the 4 bkl and pull tight.
Use a red colour pencil to add a bit of colour to the cheeks.

Nose: Embroider the nose with a 6 to 8 stitches in flesh colour between the 3rd and 4th dc crocheted off together on rnd 11.

Eyes:
Use black yarn or another colour to take a crosswise stitch over 2 to 3 dc on rnd 12, then curve the stitch up or down and hold in place with another small stitch as illustrated. Use yarn of a different colour to make a small stitch for the eye shadow.

Ears: Pink, close rnd with 1 sl st.
1: 6 dc into a thread ring.
2: 1 ch, 4x inc 1, 2 dc [10 sts].
3: 1 ch, 2x dec 1, 6 dc [8 sts], crochet off.

Press ears flat. Sew side edges together in centre front. Sew ears on right and left of head between the 7th and 8th rnd.

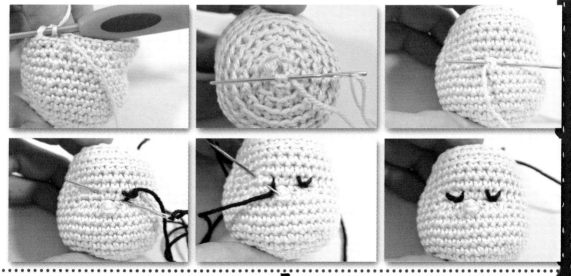

Hair:

For the hair, attach yarn to ftl of a dc on rnd 20.

Work a sl st into each ftl. If your yarn is thick, 1 sl st into every other ftl will be enough.

Work a length of ch between the sl sts. The number of ch determines the length of the hair. E.g. work less chain for the fringe. Try different chain lengths to see what you prefer (you can work up to 50 ch with cotton yarn).

Crochet the hair from rnd 20 to rnd 15 of the head. After the last dc of rnd 15, continue in back of the head between the ears. Continue to the nape of the neck.

Alternative:

If your yarn is very thick, there is no need to make lengths of chain. Just leave strands of yarn hanging for the hair and work 1 ch.

Body with Wide Skirt:

Begin with the colour for the panties.

1: 6 dc into a thread ring, close with 1 sl st.
2: 1 ch, 6x inc 1 [12 sts].
Place CT marker, continue in spiral rnds.
3: 6x (inc 1, 1 dc) [18 sts].
4: 6x (2 dc, inc 1) [24 sts].
5: 1 dc, 5x (inc 1, 3 dc), inc 1, 2 dc [30 sts].
6: 6x (4 dc, inc 1) [36 sts].
7: 2 dc, 5x (inc 1, 5 dc), inc 1, 3 dc [42 sts].
8: 6x (inc 1, 6 dc) [48 sts].
9: 4 dc, 5x (inc 1, 7 dc), inc 1, 3 dc [54 sts].

10: 6x (inc 1, 8 dc) [60 sts].
11: 5 dc, 5x (inc 1, 9 dc), inc 1, 4 dc [66 sts].
12: 4x (inc 1, 15 dc), 2 dc [70 sts].
13: 2x (inc 1, 34 dc) [72 sts].
14 to 15: 72 dc.
16: 71 dc, 1 sl st [72 sts].
The panties are now complete. Change colour: colour for upper body or for dress.
17: 1 ch, 72 dc, close with 1 sl st.
18: Work into bkl only; 1 ch, 2x (2 dc, dec 1),
    57 dc, dec 1, 2 dc, dec 1, 1 dc [68 sts].
Place CT marker, continue in spiral rnds.

19: dec 1, 11 dc, 3x (dec 1, 12 dc), dec 1, 11 dc [63 sts].
20: 5 dc, 4x (dec 1, 11 dc), dec 1, 4 dc [58 sts].
21: 3x (dec 1, 4 dc), 22 dc, 3x (dec 1, 4 dc) [52 sts].
22: 3x (3 dc, dec 1), 22 dc, 3x (3 dc, dec 1) [46 sts].
23: 5x (dec 1, 6 dc), dec 1, 4 dc [40 sts].
24: 3 dc, 4x (dec 1, 6 dc), dec 1, 3 dc [35 sts].
25: 5x (dec 1, 5 dc) [30 sts].
26: 3 dc, 2x (dec 1, 8 dc), dec 1, 5 dc [27 sts].
27: Work into ftl only; inc 1, 26 dc [28 sts].

28: 27 dc, 1 sl st [28 sts].
Change colour: flesh colour, close rnds from here with 1 sl st.
29: Work into bkl only; 1 ch, 28 dc.
30: 1 ch, 28 dc.
31: 1 ch, 5 dc, 3x dec 1, 8 dc, 3x dec 1, 3 dc [22 sts].
32: 1 ch, 2 dc, 4x dec 1, 3 dc, 4x dec 1, 1 dc [14 sts], insert filling.
33: 1 ch, 7x dec 1.
Crochet off, stuff firmly with filling. CT is on the back of the body.

Wide Skirt:

Work in the colour for the skirt/dress.
You can begin the skirt starting after rnd 20 of the body. Attach the yarn to the back of the body into ftl of a stitch on rnd 17. Hold the body so that the neck is toward you.

Close all rnds with 1 sl st.
1: 1 ch, 18x (3 dc, inc 1) [90 sts].
2: 1 ch, 18x (inc 1, 4 dc) [108 sts].
3: 1 ch, 18x (inc 1, 5 dc) [126 sts].
4: 1 ch, 18x (inc 1, 6 dc) [144 sts].
Crochet off.

Body with Narrow Skirt:

Work in the colour of the dress (= colour of panties)
1: 6 dc into a thread ring, close with 1 sl st.
2: 1 ch, 6x inc 1 [12 sts].
Place CT marker, continue in spiral rnds.
3: 6x (inc 1, 1 dc) [18 sts].
4: 6x (2 dc, inc 1) [24 sts].
5: 1 dc, 5x (inc 1, 3 dc), inc 1, 2 dc [30 sts].
6: 6x (4 dc, inc 1) [36 sts].
7: 2 dc, 5x (inc 1, 5 dc), inc 1, 3 dc [42 sts].
8: 6x (inc 1, 6 dc) [48 sts].
9: 4 dc, 5x (inc 1, 7 dc), inc 1, 3 dc [54 sts].
10: 6x (inc 1, 8 dc) [60 sts].
11: 5 dc, 5x (inc 1, 9 dc), inc 1, 4 dc [66 sts].
12: 4x (inc 1, 15 dc), 2 dc [70 sts].
13: inc 1, 34 dc, inc 1, 34 dc [72 sts].
14 to 17: 72 dc.
18: 2x (2 dc, dec 1), 57 dc, dec 1, 2 dc, dec 1, 1 dc [68 sts].
19: dec 1, 11 dc, 3x (dec 1, 12 dc), dec 1, 11 dc [63 sts].

20: 5 dc, 4x (dec 1, 11 dc), dec 1, 4 dc [58 sts].
21: 3x (dec 1, 4 dc), 22 dc, 3x (dec 1, 4 dc) [52 sts].
22: 3x (3 dc, dec 1), 22 dc, 3x (3 dc, dec 1) [46 sts].
23: 5x (dec 1, 6 dc), dec 1, 4 dc [40 sts].
24: 3 dc, 4x (dec 1, 6 dc), dec 1, 3 dc [35 sts].
25: 5x (dec 1, 5 dc) [30 sts].
26: 3 dc, 2x (dec 1, 8 dc), dec 1, 5 dc [27 sts].
27: Work into ftl only; inc 1, 26 dc [28 sts].
28: 27 dc, 1 sl st [28 sts].
Change colour: flesh colour, close rnds from here with 1 st st.
29: work into bkl only; 1 ch, 28 dc.
30: 1 ch, 28 dc.
31: 1 ch, 5 dc, 3x dec 1, 8 dc, 3x dec 1, 3 dc [22 sts].
32: 1 ch, 2 dc, 4x dec 1, 3 dc, 4x dec 1, 1 dc [14 sts], insert filling.
33: 1 ch, 7x dec 1.
Crochet off, stuff firmly with filling.
CT is on the back of the body.

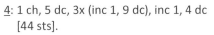

Narrow Skirt:

Work in the colour for the skirt/dress.

1: 36 ch, close with 1 sl st.
2: 1 ch, 36 dc, close rnd with 1 sl st.
3: 4x (inc 1, 8 dc) [40 sts].

4: 1 ch, 5 dc, 3x (inc 1, 9 dc), inc 1, 4 dc
   [44 sts].
5: 1 ch, 4x (inc 1, 10 dc) [48 sts].
Crochet off.
Slip skirt piece up over the legs (narrow edge at
the bottom), sew to ftl of stitches.

Bust: flesh colour, close rnd with 1 sl st.

1: 6 dc into a thread ring.
2: 1 ch, 6x inc 1 [12 sts].
3: 1 ch, 3 dc, inc 1, 8 dc [13 sts].
4: 1 ch, 3 dc, 3 dc in 1 st, 9 dc [15 sts].
5: 1 ch, 3 dc, 3 dc in 1 st, 6 dc, dec 1, 3 dc [16 sts].
Crochet off, insert filling.
Connect bust pieces in the middle. Pin bust to upper body to check the placement,
then sew in place in the ftl of the sts on rnd 5.

Top of Dress (Front): Work in the colour of the dress / bikini top.

Work back and forth in rows, turn the work at the end of each row.

1: 13 ch.
2: 1 dc into 2nd ch, 1 dc, 1 tr, 3 tr in 1, 4 tr, 3 tr in 1, 1 tr, 2 dc [16 sts].
3: 1 ch, 2 dc, 1 tr, 2x (2 tr in 1), 1 tr, 4 dc, 1 tr, 2x (2 tr in 1), 1 tr, 2 dc [20 sts].
4: 1 ch, 2 dc, 16 tr, 2 dc [20 sts].
5: 1 ch, 2 dc, 1 tr, 2x (2 tr crocheted off together), 1 tr, 4 dc, 1 tr, 2x (2 tr crocheted off together),
   1 tr, 2 dc [16 sts].
Crochet off.
Sew the underside of the top to the body at the sides and below the bust.

Straight Arms and Hands (2x):

Flesh colour, begin with a hand.

1: 6 dc into a thread ring, close with 1 sl st.
2: 1 ch, 6 dc, close with 1 sl st.
3: 1 ch, 1 dc, 3 htr in 1 st, 2x dec 1 [6 sts], close with 1 sl st.
Continue in flesh colour for a uncovered arm; change to another colour for a sleeve.
4: work into ftl only; 1 ch, 1 dc, inc 1, 2 dc, inc 1, 1 dc [8 sts].
Place CT marker, continue in spiral rnds.

Bent Arms and Hands (2x):

Flesh colour, begin with a hand.

1 to 9: See straight arm.
10: 5 dc, 2x inc 1, 4 dc, 6 ch.
11: skip 4 dc, continue from 5th dc from hook, begin rnd 11 here: 5 dc, inc 1, 4 dc, 8 ch.
12: skip 6 dc (= the 1st dc of rnd 10, the 4 unworked sts of rnd 9, the 1st dc of rnd 11); 2 dc, inc 1, 4 dc, inc 1, 1 dc, 10 ch.
13: skip 8 dc (= the 1st dc of rnd 11, the dc left unworked on rnd 12, the 1st dc of rnd 12):

5: 2 dc, inc 1, 5 dc [9 sts].
6: 3 dc, inc 1, 5 dc [10 sts].
7: 4 dc, inc 1, 5 dc [11 sts].
8: 4 dc, inc 1, 6 dc [12 sts].
9: 5 dc, inc 1, 6 dc [13 sts].
10: 5 dc, 2x inc 1, 4 dc, dec 1 [14 sts].
11: dec 1, 2 dc, inc 1, 2 dc, inc 1, 2 dc, inc 1, 3 dc [16 sts].
12: 2 dc, inc 1, 10 dc, inc 1, 2 dc [18 sts].
13 to 16: 18 dc.
17: dec 1, 14 dc, dec 1 [16 sts].
18: dec 1, 12 dc, dec 1 [14 sts].
Crochet off and insert filling.

10 dc, continue as follows over the unworked sts of the previous rnd: 1 dc in rnd 11, 1 dc in rnd 10, into ftl of rnd 9: (1 dc, 2x inc 1, 1 dc), 1 dc on rnd 10, 1 dc on rnd 12, place CT marker here [20 sts].
14: 4 dc, dec 1, 14 dc [19 sts].
15+16: 19 dc.
17: 4 dc, dec 1, 13 dc [18 sts].
18+19: 18 dc.
20: 2 dc, dec 1, 1 dc, dec 1, 11 dc [16 sts].
21: dec 1, 3 dc, dec 1, 9 dc [14 sts].
Crochet off and insert filling.

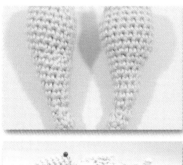

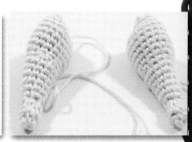

Place the arms on the right and left side of the body, sewing rnd 18 almost completely flat to the body. Note: Once rnd 18 has been sewn in place, the arm position can no longer be adjusted. How to sew on the arm depends on the desired pose of the lady.

E.g. should the lady hold a cup of coffee, pull the inside of the arm toward the body with a thread at bust level.

Bent Legs for Sitting Lady:

Both legs are worked exactly the same. Begin with the colour for the shoe:

1: 5 ch.

2: 3 dc into 2nd ch, 3 dc, now continue on the other side of the 5 ch foundation, 3 dc into 1st ch, 3 dc, close with 1 sl st [12 sts].

3: Crochet into the bkl only; 1 ch, 4 dc, 4 tr crocheted off together, 4 dc [9 sts], close with 1 sl st.

Change colour: flesh colour.

4: Crochet into the bkl only; 1 ch, 2 dc, 2x dec 1, 3 dc, work 1 more dc (= 1st dc of rnd 4).

Place CT marker and continue in spiral rnds.

5: 5 dc, 2x inc 1 [9 sts].

6: 6 dc, 2x inc 1, 1 dc [11 sts].

7: 7 dc, 2x inc 1, 2 dc [13 sts].

8: 7 dc, inc 1, 4 dc, inc 1 [15 sts].

9: 11 dc, inc 1, 3 dc [16 sts].

10+11: 16 dc.

12: 3 dc, inc 1, 1 dc, inc 1, 4 dc, 10 ch, skip 6 dc and continue from 7th dc from hook.

13: 5 dc, inc 1, 5 dc, 12 ch.

14: skip 8 dc (= 1 dc of rnd 12, 6 dc of rnd 11, 1 dc of rnd 13) and continue from 2nd dc of rnd 13; 10 dc, 12 ch.

15: 10 dc into 10 dc of rnd 14, 12 ch.

16 skip 10 dc (= 1 dc of rnd 13, 1 dc of rnd 12, 6 dc of rnd 11, 1 dc of rnd 13, 1 dc of rnd 15), 2 dc, dec 1, 1 dc, dec 1, 2 dc, continue with the 14 dc at side edges and the dc not worked on the last rnd as follows (the loose lengths of chain should lie in back/inside); 1 dc into side edge of rnd 15, 1 dc into rnd 13, 1 dc into rnd 12, work into ftl of the 6 dc of rnd 11 (1 dc, inc 1, 2 dc, inc 1, 1 dc), 1 dc into rnd 13, 1 dc into side edge of rnd 14, 1 dc into rnd 15, place CT marker [21 sts].

17: 3 dc, dec 1, 3 dc, inc 1, 3 dc, 6 ch, skip 4 dc, into 5th dc from hook, 4 dc, inc 1

18: 9 dc, inc 1, 1 dc, 10 ch, skip 6 dc (= 1 dc of rnd 17, 4 dc of rnd 16, 1 dc of rnd 17), 5 dc.

19: inc 1, 5 dc, inc 1, 5 dc , 1 dc into rnd 17, (1 dc, 2x inc 1, 1 dc) into rnd 16, 1 dc into rnd 17, 1 dc, inc 1, 2 dc, 1 sl st [28 sts].

Change colour: colour of panties.

20: 1 ch, 7x (3 dc, inc 1)
Crochet off.

If you are not sure how to crochet half-rounds, see the You Tube film at my website.
In dutch or german language only.
Dutch: www.haakpret.nl - button Download and the picture with the lady-leg.
German: www.haekelfreude.de - button Download grundtechniken and the picture with the lady-leg.

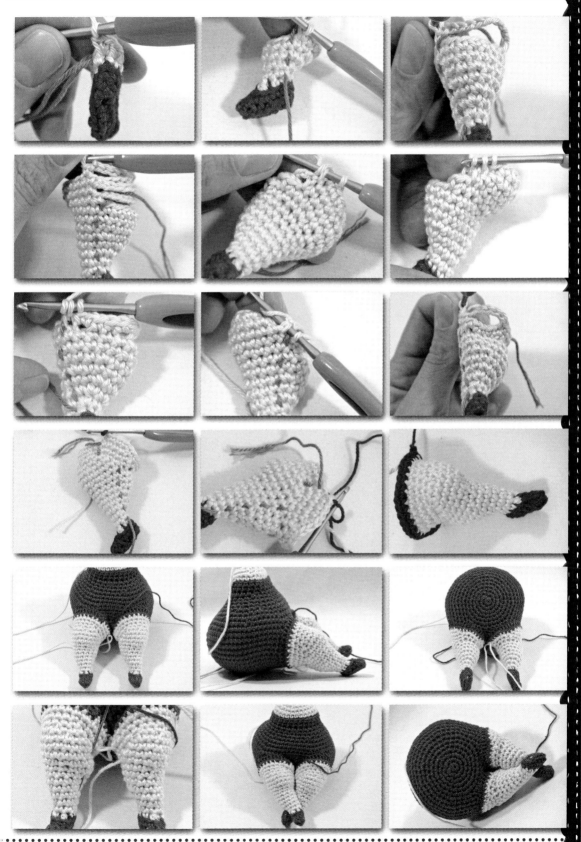

Sitting Position of the Lady:

Lay the legs next to each other on the lower edge of the body and crochet into place through the ftl on rnds 7 to 17, stretching upper edge of legs. Then join the inside of the legs together at the crotch with 3 dc.

There are different possibilites of sewing the legs together:
– Cross the legs at the bottom. The knees should point a bit outward when attaching the legs.
– One foot lies on the knee of the other leg. The knee of one leg should point a bit outward when attaching the legs (lay the foot of this leg on the knee).
For best results, first check the position of the legs before attaching them.

Straight Legs for the Standing Lady:

The right and left legs are crocheted differently.

Right Leg:

Begin with the colour for the shoe:
1: 5 ch.
2: 3 dc into 2nd ch, 3 dc, now continue on the other side of the 5 ch foundation, 3 dc into 1st ch, 3 dc, close with 1 sl st [12 sts].
3: Work into bkl only; 1 ch, 4 dc, 4 tr crochet off together, 4 dc [9 sts], close with 1 sl st.
Change colour: flesh colour or the colour of the panties.
4: Work into bkl only; 1 ch, 2 dc, 2x dec 1, 3 dc, work 1 more dc (into 1st dc of rnd 4).
Place CT marker, continue in spiral rnds.
5: 5 dc, 2x inc 1 [9 sts].
6: 7 dc, 2x inc 1 [11 sts].
7: 8 dc, 2x inc 1, 1 dc [13 sts].
8: 7 dc, inc 1, 4 dc, inc 1 [15 sts].
9: 11 dc, inc 1, 3 dc [16 sts].
10 + 11: 16 dc.

12: 12 dc, dec 1, 2 dc [15 sts].
13: 4 dc, inc 1, 1 dc, inc 1, 8 dc [17 sts].
14: 6 dc, inc 1, 10 dc [18 sts].
15: 14 dc, work into ftl: 4x inc 1 [22 sts].
16: 2 dc, inc 1, 8 dc, inc 1, 4 dc, inc 1, 2 dc, inc 1, 2 dc [26 sts].
IMPORTANT: From here always work the under-lined sl st into ftl.
17: 6 sl st, 1 dc, inc 1, 5 dc, inc 1, 6 dc, inc 1, 5 dc [29 sts].
18: 6 sl st into the sl st of rnd 17, 2 dc, inc 1, 2 dc, inc 1, 5 dc, inc 1, 3 dc, inc 1, 3 dc, inc 1, 3 sl st [34 sts].
Change colour: colour for the panties.
19: 6 sl st into sl st of rnd 18, 3 sl st, 5x (3 dc, inc 1), 2 dc, 3 sl st, close rnd with 1 sl st [39 sts].
Crochet off.

Left Leg:

Begin with the colour for the shoe:
1: 5 ch.
2: 3 dc into 2nd ch, 3 dc, now continue on the other side of the 5 ch foundation, 3 dc into 1st ch, 3 dc, close with 1 sl st [12 sts].
3: Work into bkl only; 1 ch, 4 dc, 4 tr crocheted off together, 4 dc [9 sts], close rnd with 1 sl st.
Change colour: flesh colour or the colour of the panties.
4: Work into bkl only; 1 ch, 2 dc, 2x dec 1, 3 dc, work 1 more dc (into 1st dc of rnd 4).
Place CT marker, continue in spiral rnds.
5: 5 dc, 2x inc 1 [9 sts].

6: 7 dc, 2x inc 1 [11 sts].
7: 8 dc, 2x inc 1, 1 dc [13 sts].
8: 7 dc, inc 1, 4 dc, inc 1 [15 sts].
9: 11 dc, inc 1, 3 dc [16 sts].
10 + 11: 16 dc.
12: 12 dc, dec 1, 2 dc [15 sts].
13: 3 dc, inc 1, 1 dc, inc 1, 9 dc [17 sts].
14: 5 dc, inc 1, 11 dc [18 sts].
15: 14 dc, work into ftl: 4x inc 1 [22 sts].
16: 2 dc, inc 1, 8 dc, inc 1, 4 dc, inc 1, 2 dc, inc 1, 2 dc [26 sts].
IMPORTANT: From here always work the under-lined sl st into ftl.

17: 4 dc, inc 1, 5 dc, inc 1, 1 dc, 6 sl st, 5 dc, inc 1, 2 dc [29 sts].

18: 2 dc, inc 1, 3 dc, inc 1, 3 dc, inc 1, 3 sl st, 6 sl st into sl st of rnd 17, 2 dc, inc 1, 2 dc, inc 1, 2 dc, 1 sl st

[34 sts]. Change colour: panties.

19: 1 ch, 2 dc, 3x (inc 1, 3 dc), 1 sl st, 9 sl st into sl st of rnd 18, 3 sl st, 2 dc, inc 1, 3 dc, inc 1, close rnd with 1 sl st [39]. Crochet off.

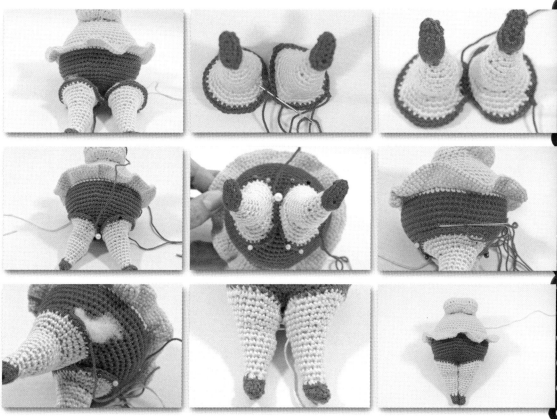

Sew legs together at centre 4th and 5th ftl. IMPORTANT: Check the position of the feet, the toes should point forward. Pin the last rnd of the legs centred on underside of body, stretched to fit. Sew on the legs, catching just the front loop of each stitch. The legs reach to rnd 11 of the body at the sides. Insert filling into legs just before closing the seam. Join inside of legs together with a bit of flesh coloured yarn and a few stitches.

See the gentleman in the evening suit for further illustrations for the straight legs, on pages 41 to 43.

COFFEE TIME

COFFEE TIME:

Follow the basic instructions to crochet the ladies.
The ladies can be crocheted with a narrow skirt or with a wide skirt.
The arms and legs can be varied as you like.
If the ladies should be sitting, crochet bent legs: see page 12. Cross the legs at the ankles or cross one leg over the other at the knee. Sew legs together.
These three ladies have straight arms. If the arms are sewn to the cup and the saucer (optional: also at the sides of the body), they can still be slightly bent.

Lady on the left, in the red dress:
Narrow skirt. Use the same colour for the panties and for the dress, there is no need to change colours.
Crochet the hair with sl st and 1 strand of Firenze colour 12 (there are no lengths of chain).

Lady in the middle, in the pink dress:
Wide skirt. Crochet the panties and the shoes in dark pink. For the torso light pink is used.
Crochet the hair with sl st and 1 strand of Firenze colour 11 (there are no lengths of chain).

Lady on the right, in the orange dress:
Wide skirt. Crochet the panties with orange, shoes and polka dots with yellow.
Crochet the hair with sl st and lengths of chain with cotton yarn Larra in light yellow.

Lady in the dark blue dress with white polka dots:
Narrow skirt. Use the same colour for the panties and for the dress (there is no need to change colours).
Crochet the hair with sl st and lengths of chain with cotton yarn Larra in brown.

Polka dots on the blue dress: White.

Work with 1 strand of yarn. Exit the needle where a polka dot is to be embroidered.
Work a French knot for each dot as follows: Exit the needle, insert into the same place and exit 1 dc next to this again. Wrap the thread around the point of the needle 3 to 4 times. Insert needle into the first point of exit again, pushing the thread down to form a knot. Exit the needle where the next dot should be.

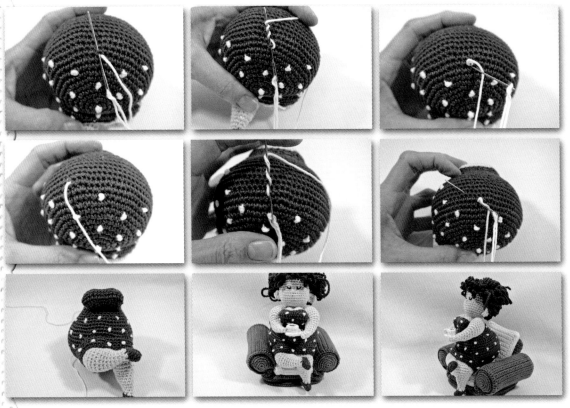

Polka dots on the panties and dress: Use the colour of your choice. Make any number of dots as you like. Crochet the polka dots as follows:

1: 6 dc into a thread ring, close with 1 sl st. Crochet off.
Use the end of the thread to sew the dot to the panties or dress through the bkl of the stitches.

Coffee cup with saucer:

Saucer: <u>White</u>, close rnd with 1 sl st.
<u>1</u>: 6 dc into a thread ring.
<u>2</u>: 1 ch, 6x inc 1 [12 sts].
<u>3</u>: Work into bkl; 1 ch, 12 dc.
Crochet off.

Coffee: <u>Dark brown</u>, close rnd with 1 sl st.
<u>1</u>: 9 dc into a thread ring.
Crochet off.

Coffee cup: <u>White</u>, close rnd with 1 sl st.
<u>1</u>: 6 dc into a thread ring
<u>2</u>: 1 ch, 3x (inc 1, 1 dc) [9 sts].
<u>3</u>: 1 ch, 9 dc.
Work the coffee into the cup (9 ftl on rnd 1) together with the dc of rnd 3 on the cup,
insert the hook first through the dc of rnd 3, then into ftl of the coffee.
<u>4</u>: 1 ch, 9 dc, 6 ch.
Crochet off.
Sew on the 6th ch of rnd 4 to form a handle.

Sew the cup to the saucer. Then sew the saucer with the cup between the hands of the lady.

Earrings:
Attach thread to back of one ear, exit needle in front. Work a French knot for the earring
(like for the small polka dots), wrapping the thread around the point of the needle 5 times.
Insert needle into ear again, conceal thread.

GREY ARMCHAIR

GREY ARMCHAIR

Crochet the following pieces for the armchair:
– bottom piece to lower edge of seat + chair back (to cushion) 1x
– seat (under cushion) 1x
– circles for front and back of armrests 4x
– armrest 2x
– seat cushion 1x
– back cushion 1x

Bottom Piece + Chair Back:

Begin with the bottom piece, use the colour of your choice (will not be visible on the finished chair until round 16).
1: 8 dc into a thread ring, close with 1 sl st.
2: 1 ch, 4x (1 dc, 3 dc in 1 st) [16 sts].
Place CT marker, continue in spiral rnds.
3: 2 dc, 3x (3 dc in 1 st, 3 dc), 3 dc in 1 st, 1 dc [24 sts].
4: 4 dc, 3x (inc 1, 5 dc), inc 1, 1 dc [28 sts].
5: 4 dc, 3x (3 dc in 1 st, 6 dc), 3 dc in 1 st, 2 dc [36 sts].
6: 5 dc, 3x (3 dc in 1 st, 8 dc), 3 dc in 1 st, 3 dc [44 sts].
7: 7 dc, 3x (inc 1, 10 dc), inc 1, 3 dc [48 sts].
8: 7 dc, 3x (3 dc in 1 st, 11 dc), 3 dc in 1 st, 4 dc [56 sts].
9: 8 dc, 3x (3 dc in 1 st, 13 dc), 3 dc in 1 st, 5 dc [64 sts].
10: 10 dc, 3x (inc 1, 15 dc), inc 1, 5 dc [68 sts].
11: 10 dc, 3x (3 dc in 1 st, 16 dc), 3 dc in 1 st, 6 dc [76 sts].
12: 11 dc, 3x (3 dc in 1 st, 18 dc), 3 dc in 1 st, 7 dc [84 sts].
13: 12 dc, 3x (3 dc in 1 st, 20 dc), 3 dc in 1 st, 8 dc [92 sts].
14: 14 dc, 3x (inc 1, 22 dc), inc 1, 8 dc [96 sts].
15: 14 dc, 3x (3 dc in 1 st, 23 dc), 3 dc in 1 st, 8 dc, 1 sl st [104 sts].
16: Work into ftl only; 1 ch, 104 htr, close rnd with 1 sl st.
17: Work into bkl only; 1 ch, 104 dc, close rnd with 1 sl st.
18: Work into bkl only; 1 ch, 104 htr, close rnd with 1 sl st.
19: Join the bkl of rnd 18 with the bkl of the dc on rnd 15; 1 ch, 104 dc, close rnd with 1 sl st.

20: 1 ch, 104 dc.
Place CT marker, continue in spiral rnds.
21 to 23: 104 dc.
24: Crochet the edge between the side pieces over the middle 18 dc in centre front as follows: work 10 dc into ftl, 4 dc into both loops of stitches to first corner (place one CT marker), 26 dc to 2nd corner (place another CT marker), 4 dc, work into ftl; 1 ch, 18 htr. Turn.
25: Work into ftl; 1 ch, 18 dc, TURN.
26: Work into bkl; 1 ch, 18 htr.
Now continue from 1st dc of rnd 23:
27: Work into both loops of stitches; 4 dc to 3rd corner (place a new CT marker), 26 dc to 4th corner (place another CT marker), 4 dc, working into ftl only; 8 dc.
28: 14 dc to 1st corner, 26 dc to 2nd corner, 4 dc, now join the bkl of the htr on rnd 26 with the opposite lying bkl of the 18 dc on rnd 23, 18 dc, 4 dc to 3rd corner, 26 dc to 4th corner, 12 dc [104 sts].
29: 14 dc to corner, 26 dc to corner, 4 dc, TURN.
Now work in rows back and forth and TURN at the end of each row.
30 to 32: 1 ch, 86 dc.
33: 1 ch, 52 dc.

Crochet the chair back from here:
34 to 43: 1 ch, 18 dc.
44: (The inside of the work faces you. The right side of the armchair now lies in back); work into bkl only; 1 ch, 18 dc.
45: Join the bkl of the dc on rnd 44 with the opposite lying ftl of the dc on rnd 43; 1 ch, 18 dc.

46: Work into ftl only; 1 ch, 18 dc.

47: 1 ch, 18 dc.

48: The inside of the work faces you. The right side now lies in back. Work into bkl only; 1 ch, 18 dc.

49: Join the bkl of the dc on rnd 48 with the opposite lying ftl of the dc on rnd 49; 1 ch, 18 dc, 4 ch.

50: Work 1 dc in the 2nd ch, 2 dc into ftl; 18 dc, 4 ch.

51: 1 dc in the 2nd ch, 2 dc, 21 dc.

52 to 67: 1 ch, 24 dc.

Crochet off.

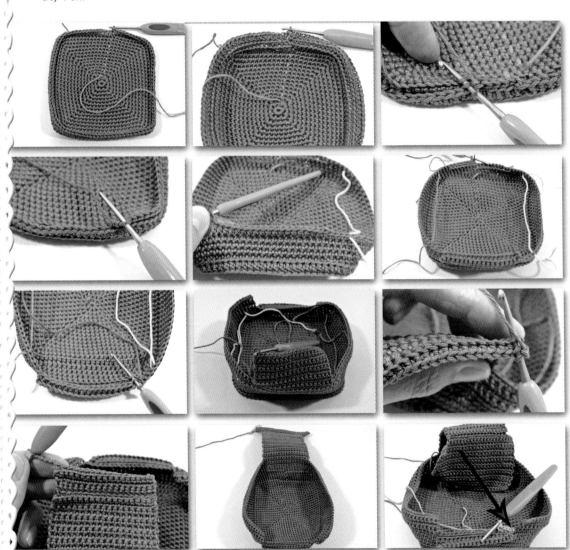

Seat under Seat Cushion:

Colour of your choice.

Attach yarn to 1st dc of the middle 18 dc on rnd 28 in front between both side pieces (see blue arrow, illustration below right).

TURN at the end of each row.

1 to 26: 1 ch, 18 dc.

Crochet off.

Circles for Armrests (4x):

1: 6 dc into a thread ring, close with 1 sl st.
2: 1 ch, 6x inc 1 [12 sts].
Place CT marker, continue in spiral rnds.

3: 6x (inc 1, 1 dc) [18 sts].
4: 6x (2 dc, inc 1) [24 sts].
5: 1 dc, 5x (inc 1, 3 dc), inc 1, 2 dc [30 sts].
6: 2 dc, 4x (inc 1, 6 dc) [34 sts].
Crochet off.

Armrests:

Left Armrest: (left side when seated in the chair):

Crochet onto left side of seat, attach yarn to 1st dc of rnd 1 (front).
1: crochet into the ends of the 26 rows, 1 dc into end of each row; 1 ch, 26 dc.
2 to 34: 1 ch, 26 dc.
End in front after row 34, do not crochet off, but continue.
Join front of armrest with a circle as follows:
Work 1 dc each into end of rows 34 to 5 [= 30 dc] and into bkl of each dc on rnd 6 of the circle;
the last 4 row ends of the armrest and the last 4 dc of the circle remain (the seam will be closed later): 1 ch, 30 dc.
Crochet off.

Now join the back of the armrest with a circle likewise as instructed above, but first attach the yarn to the last dc of row 34 on the armrest and crochet into bkl of each dc on rnd 6 of the circle: 1 ch, 30 dc (to rnd 5 of the armrest).
Crochet off.

Right Armrest: (right side when seated in the chair):

Crochet onto right side of seat, attach yarn to last dc of rnd 26 (back).
1: crochet into the ends of the 26 rows, 1 dc into end of each row; 1 ch, 26 dc.
2 to 34: 1 ch, 26 dc.
End in back after row 34, do not crochet off, but continue.
Join back of armrest with a circle as follows:
Work 1 dc into end of rows 34 to 5 [= 30 dc] and into bkl of each dc on rnd 6 of the circle;
the last 4 row ends of the armrest and the last 4 dc of the circle remain (the seam will be closed later): 1 ch, 30 dc.
Crochet off.
Now join the front of the armrest with a circle likewise as instructed above, but first attach the yarn to the last dc of row 34 of the armrest and crochet into ftl of each 6 of the circle: 1 ch, 30 dc (to rnd 5 of the armrest).
Crochet off.

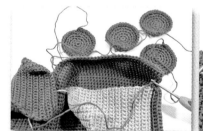

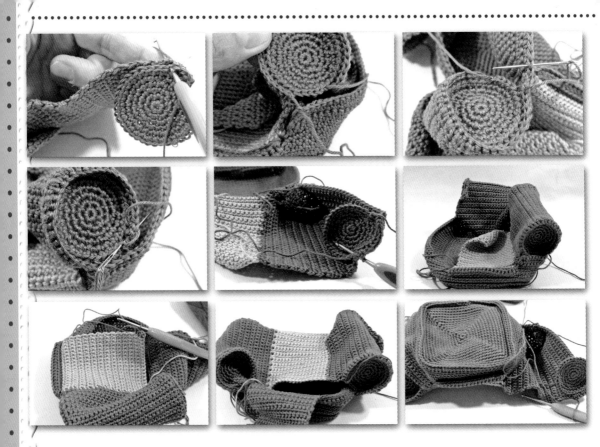

Foam Filling for the Seat, Chair Back and Armrests:

Measure the entire width of the seat on the bottom piece. Measure the width of the seat between the armrests. Subtract these measurements one from the other = height of both armrests.

Foam Filling for the Seat:
Width: width of seat minus width of both armrests.
Depth: from front to chair back.
Height: lower edge to upper edge of bottom piece.
Lay the foam filling inside the crochet piece and join the seat with rnd 26 to the chair back at the loops of the chair back left unworked (dc on rnd 23).
The space to the right and left of the seat will be filled with the foam filling for the armrests.

Foam Filling for the Chair Back:
Height: from rnd 28 of the seam to the edges on rnds 45 and 49.
Width: armchair 18 dc, sofa 59 dc.
Depth: measurement between rnds 45 and 49.
Lay the foam filling inside the crochet piece and close the side edges of the chair back: Crochet the side pieces to front of chair back from 3 dc on the left and right. Sew rnd 67 to the seat at the centre 18 dc [56 sts] between rnds 22 and 23.

Foam Filling for the Armrests (2x):

Cut two long strips to place vertically into the bottom piece to the right and left of the seat. The strips are then rolled up and placed inside the armrests (see also page 29).
Width: depth of seat.
Length: approx. 2x the depth of the seat (the correct length will be determined later).
Height: width of bottom minus width of seat, divided by 2.

Place one strip into the bottom piece vertically to the right / left of the seat, roll up the other end and place inside the armrest. Rnd 34 of the armrest should now meet with rnd 28 [29] of the side piece. If the strip is too long, it can be shortened to fit.
Close the seam of the armrest: join 28 dc of rnd 34 with the centre 28 dc of rnd 28 [29], do not join the 4 dc to the right and left, these stitches will be closed separately.
Now take stitches back and forth with needle and thread between rnd 34 and rnd 28 [29], to completely sew on the piece, but do not pull the thread too tightly.

If you place cushions on the armchair or sofa, the total height may then be too much. The seat can be made flatter by joining it to the bottom with needle and thread. Take care to retain the shape of the chair or sofa.

See page 29 for illustrations on finishing the armchair.

Seat Cushion: Turn at the end of each row.

1: 17 ch.
2: 1 dc into 2nd ch, 15 dc [16 sts].
3 to 21: 1 ch, 16 dc, then continue in rnds:
22: 1 ch, into end of rows 21 to 2; 3 dc in 1 st, 18 dc, 3 dc in 1 st; into st of row 1: 16 dc; into end of rows 2 to 21; 3 dc in 1 st, 18 dc, 3 dc in 1 st; into stitch of row 21: 16 dc [80 sts].
Place CT marker, continue in spiral rnds.
23: Work into bkl only; 3 dc crocheted off together, 18 dc, 3 dc crocheted off together, 16 dc, 3 dc crocheted off together, 18 dc, 3 dc crocheted off together, 16 dc [72 sts].

24: 1 dc, 3 dc in 1 st, 18 dc, 3 dc in 1 st, 16 dc, 3 dc in 1 st, 18 dc, 3 dc in 1 st, 15 dc [80 sts].
25: Work into bkl only; 1 dc, 3 dc crocheted off together, 18 dc, 3 dc crocheted off together, 16 dc, 3 dc crocheted off together, 18 dc, 3 dc crocheted off together, 15 dc [72 sts], work 1 more dc after CT, TURN.
From here, turn at end of each row.
26 to 45: 1 ch, 16 dc. Crochet off.
Sew top to side edges on row 25. Stuff cushion lightly.

Chair Back Cushion: Turn after every row.

1: 17 ch.
2: 1 dc into 2nd ch, 15 dc [16 sts].
3 to 17: 1 ch, 16 dc, then continue in rnds:
18: 1 ch, into end of rows 17 to 2; 3 dc in 1 st, 14 dc, 3 dc in 1 st; in the st of rnd 1: 16 dc; into end of rnds 2 to 17; 3 dc in 1 st, 14 dc, 3 dc in 1 st, into st of row 17; 16 dc [72 sts].
Place CT marker, continue in spiral rnds.
19: Work into bkl only; 3 dc crocheted off together, 14 dc, 3 dc crocheted off together, 16 dc, 3 dc crocheted off together, 14 dc, 3 dc crocheted off together, 16 dc [64 sts].

20: 1 dc, 3 dc in 1 st, 14 dc, 3 dc in 1 st, 16 dc, 3 dc in 1 st, 14 dc, 3 dc in 1 st, 15 dc [72 sts].
21: Work into bkl only; 1 dc, 3 dc crocheted off together, 14 dc, 3 dc crocheted off together, 16 dc, 3 dc crocheted off together, 14 dc, 3 dc crocheted off together, 64 dc [72 sts], work 1 more dc after CT, TURN.
From here, turn at end of each row.
22 to 37: 1 ch, 16 dc. Crochet off.
Sew top to side edges on row 21. Stuff cushion lightly.

SOFA

SOFA:

Crochet the following pieces for the sofa:
– bottom piece to lower edge of seat + sofa back (to cushions) 1x
– seat (under cushion) 1x
– circles for front and back of armrests 4x
– armrest 2x
– seat cushion 3x
– back cushion 3x

Bottom Piece + Sofa Back:

Begin with the bottom piece, use the colour of your choice (will not be visible on the finished sofa until round 16).

1: 44 ch, worked loosely.
2: 3 dc into 2nd ch from hook, 42 dc, continue on the other side of the 44 foundation chain, 3 dc into 1st ch, 42 dc [90 sts].
Place CT marker, continue in spiral rnds.
3: 3 dc in 1 st, 1 dc, 3 dc in 1 st, 42 dc, 3 dc in 1 st, 1 dc, 3 dc in 1 st, 42 dc [98 sts].
4: 1 dc, 2 dc in 1 st, 3 dc, 2 dc in 1 st, 44 dc, 2 dc in 1 st, 3 dc, 2 dc in 1 st, 43 dc [102 sts].
5: 2 dc, 3 dc in 1 st, 3 dc, 3 dc in 1 st, 46 dc, 3 dc in 1 st, 3 dc, 3 dc in 1 st, 44 dc [110 sts].
6: 3 dc, 2 dc in 1 st, 6 dc, 2 dc in 1 st, 47 dc, 2 dc in 1 st, 6 dc, 2 dc in 1 st, 44 dc [114 sts].
7: 3 dc, 3 dc in 1 st, 7 dc, 3 dc in 1 st, 48 dc, 3 dc in 1 st, 7 dc, 3 dc in 1 st, 45 dc [122 sts].
8: 5 dc, 3 dc in 1 st, 9 dc, 3 dc in 1 st, 50 dc, 3 dc in 1 st, 9 dc– 3 dc in 1 st, 45 dc [130 sts].
9: 6 dc, 3 dc in 1 st, 11 dc, 3 dc in 1 st, 52 dc, 3 dc in 1 st, 11 dc– 3 dc in 1 st, 46 dc [138 sts].
10: 7 dc, 3 dc in 1 st, 13 dc, 3 dc in 1 st, 54 dc, 3 dc in 1 st, 13 dc, 3 dc in 1 st, 47 dc [146 sts].
11: 8 dc, 3 dc in 1 st, 15 dc, 3 dc in 1 st, 56 dc, 3 dc in 1 st, 15 dc, 3 dc in 1 st, 48 dc [154 sts].
12: 9 dc, 3 dc in 1 st, 17 dc, 3 dc in 1 st, 58 dc, 3 dc in 1 st, 17 dc, 3 dc in 1 st, 49 dc [162 sts].
13: 11 dc, 2 dc in 1 st, 18 dc, 2 dc in 1 st, 61 dc, 2 dc in 1 st, 18 dc, 2 dc in 1 st, 50 dc [166 sts].
14: 11 dc, 3 dc in 1 st, 20 dc, 3 dc in 1 st, 61 dc, 3 dc in 1 st, 20 dc, 3 dc in 1 st, 50 dc [174 sts].
15: 12 dc, 3 dc in 1 st, 22 dc, 3 dc in 1 st, 63 dc, 3 dc in 1 st, 22 dc, 3 dc in 1 st, 51 dc [182 sts].
16: 13 dc, 2 dc in 1 st, 24 dc, 2 dc in 1 st, 65 dc, 2 dc in 1 st, 24 dc, 2 dc in 1 st, 51 dc, 1 sl st [186 sts].
17: Work into ftl only; 1 ch, 186 htr, close rnd with 1 sl st.
18: Work into bkl only; 1 ch, 186 dc, close rnd with 1 sl st.
19: Work into bkl only; 1 ch, 186 htr, close rnd with 1 sl st.
20: Join bkl of the dc on rnd 19 with the bkl of the dc on rnd 16; 1 ch, 186 dc, close rnd with 1 sl st.
21: 1 ch, 186 dc.
Place CT marker, continue in spiral rnds.
22 to 24: 186 dc.
25: Work an edge on this rnd in centre front between both side pieces; work 6 dc into ftl; 6 dc into both loops of -stitches to 1st corner (place a CT marker), 25 dc to 2nd corner (place another CT marker), 6 dc into ftl; 1 ch, 56 htr, TURN.
26: Work into ftl; 1 ch, 56 dc, TURN.
27: Work into bkl; 1 ch, 56 htr.
Now work into first following stitch of rnd 24 again:
28: Work into both loops of stitches; 6 dc to 3rd corner (place a CT marker), 25 dc to 4th corner (place another CT marker), 6 dc, work into ftl only; 50 dc.
29: 43 dc, join the bkl of the htr on rnd 27 with the bkl of the 56 dc of rnd 24 lying opposite, 87 dc [186 sts].
30: 12 dc to corner, 25 dc to corner, 6 dc, TURN
TURN after every row from here.
31 to 33: 1 ch, 130 dc.
34: 1 ch, 93 dc.
Now work the sofa back:
35 to 44: 1 ch, 56 dc.

45: The inside of the work faces you. The right side of the sofa now lies in back; work into bkl only; 1 ch, 56 dc.

46: Now join the bkl of the dc on rnd 44 with the ftl of the dc on rnd 43 lying opposite; 1 ch, 56 dc.

47: Work into ftl only; 1 ch, 56 dc.

48: 1 ch, 56 dc.

49: The inside of the work faces you. The right side of the sofa now lies in back; work into bkl only; 1 ch, 56 dc.

50: Now join the bkl of the dc on rnd 48 with the ftl of the dc on rnd 47 lying opposite; 1 ch, 56 dc, 4 ch.

51: 1 dc into 2nd ch, 2 dc, work into ftl; 56 dc, 4 ch.

52: 1 dc into 2nd ch, 2 dc, 59 dc.

53 to 68: 1 ch, 62 dc. Crochet off.

Seat under Seat Cushion: Colour of your choice.
Attach yarn to 1st dc of the middle 56 dc on rnd 29 in front between both side pieces (see blue arrow, illustration below right on page 22).
TURN at the end of each row.
1 to 26: 1 ch, 56 dc.
Crochet off.

Circles for Armrests (4x): Work exactly as for armchair, see p. 23.

Armrests:

Left Armrest: (left side when seated):

Crochet onto left side of seat, attach yarn to 1st dc of rnd 1 (front).
1: crochet into the ends of the 26 rows, 1 dc into end of each row; 1 ch, 26 dc.
2 to 34: 1 ch, 26 dc.
End in front after row 34, do not crochet off, but continue.
Join front of armrest with a circle as follows:
Work 1 dc each into end of rows 34 to 5 R [= 30 dc] and into bkl of each dc on rnd 6 of the circle; the last 4 row ends of the armrest and the last 4 dc of the circle remain (the seam will be closed later): 1 ch, 30 dc.
Crochet off.

Now join the back of the armrest with a circle likewise as instructed above, but first attach the yarn to the last dc of row 34 on the armrest and crochet into bkl of each dc on rnd 6 of the circle: 1 ch, 30 dc (to rnd 5 of the armrest).
Crochet off.

Right Armrest: (right side when seated in the chair):

Crochet onto right side of seat, attach yarn to last dc of rnd 26 (back).
1: crochet into the ends of the 26 rows, 1 dc into end of each row; 1 ch, 26 dc.
2 to 34: 1 ch, 26 dc.
End in back after row 34, do not crochet off, but continue.
Join back of armrest with a circle as follows:
Work 1 dc into end of rows 34 to 5 [= 30 dc] and into bkl of each dc on rnd 6 of the circle;

the last 4 row ends of the armrest and the last 4 dc of the circle remain (the seam will be closed later): 1 ch, 30 dc. Crochet off.
Now join the front of the armrest with a circle likewise as instructed above, but first attach the yarn to the last dc of row 34 of the armrest and crochet into ftl of each 6 of the circle: 1 ch, 30 dc (to rnd 5 of the armrest).
Crochet off.

Foam Filling for the Seat, Sofa Back and Armrests:
See instructions for armchair on page 24.

Foam Filling for the Seat: See instructions for the armchair on page 24.

Foam Filling for the Sofa Back: See instructions for the armchair on page 24.

Foam Filling for the Armrests (2x): See instructions for the armchair on page 25.

Seat Cushion (3x): See instructions for the armchair on page 25.

Sofa Back Cushion (3x): See instructions for the armchair on page 25.

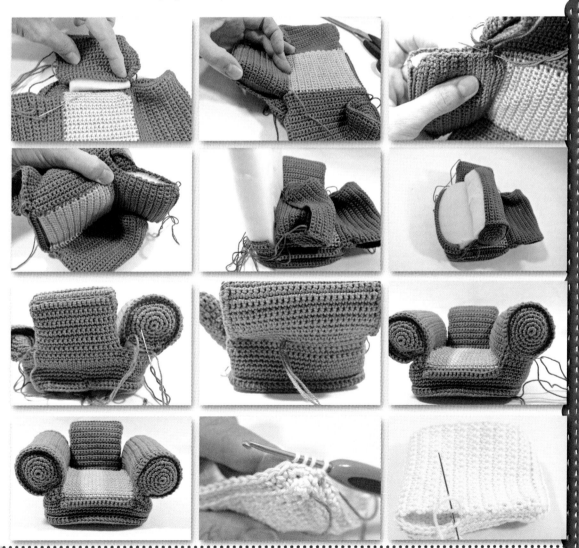

OUT FOR A WALK

OUT FOR A WALK

Follow the basic instructions to crochet the ladies. Before you begin with the body, please read the instructions: Each lady has one bent arm and one straight arm. Hook their bent arms together when they go out for a walk. You may also wish to make a bent arm to hold the handbag. When working the arm, the colour must be changed after the hand.
Choose the straight leg form for these ladies, see page 14.

In order for the ladies to stand, insert florist's wire into the legs up from underneath the grey pavement.
For the hair, use cotton yarn Larra in brown or Firenze in black. The hair is worked with lengths of chain stitch

Body:

Work rnds <u>1</u> to <u>13</u> in the colour of the panties, see basic instructions for body with narrow skirt on page 9. Crochet off. Set this piece aside. Now crochet the skirt.

Narrow Skirt:

Use the colour of your choice.
<u>1</u>: 52 ch, close with 1 sl st.
<u>2</u>: 1 ch, 52 dc.
Place CT marker and continue in spiral rnds.
<u>3</u>: inc 1, 20 dc, inc 1, 20 dc, inc 1, 9 dc [55 sts].
<u>4</u>: 10 dc, inc 1, 20 dc, inc 1, 20 dc, inc 1, 2 dc [58 sts].
<u>5</u>: 15 dc, inc 1, 28 dc, inc 1, 13 dc [60 sts].
<u>6</u>: 5 dc, inc 1, 29 dc, inc 1, 24 dc [62 sts].
<u>7</u>: 2x (inc 1, 30 dc).
<u>8</u>: 10 dc, inc 1, 31 dc, inc 1, 21 dc [66 sts].
<u>9</u>: 25 dc, inc 1, 32 dc, inc 1, 7 dc [68 sts].
<u>10</u>: 16 dc, inc 1, 33 dc, inc 1, 17 dc [70 sts].
<u>11</u>: inc 1, 34 dc, inc 1, 33 dc, 1 sl st [72 sts].

If you would like to crochet the jacket in a different colour, crochet off here and attach yarn in the new colour to continue.
If you crochet the skirt and jacket in the same colour, continue without crocheting off.
Continue the panties on the next rnd (= rnd 14) after rnd 13, catching the skirt: Lay panties behind the skirt; insert hook into both loops of the stitches for the skirt, but for the panties just into ftl.
<u>14</u>: 1 ch, 72 dc, close rnd with 1 sl st.
<u>15</u>: Work into bkl only; 1 ch, 72 dc.
Place CT marker and continue in spiral rnds.
<u>16</u> to <u>33</u>: see basic instructions for body with narrow skirt, beginning on page 9.
Stuff the body firmly with filling.

Optional: Embroider polka dots, see page 18.

Fur Trimmed Jacket: Materials and colour of your choice.
The length of the foundation ch depends on the material.
Thicker yarn requires a shorter foundation. I chose Scheepjeswol Sicilia colour number 14 for the fur trim. I used a bit of eyelash yarn I found in my bag of remnants for the pink trim.
<u>Measure the length required for the fur trim:</u>
Lay a thread along the edge beginning in centre front at the transition skirt/jacket. Run the thread around the body following the upper edge of the skirt. Then lay the thread vertically up at centre front to the upper jacket edge, and from there around the neck. End thread in centre front at upper jacket edge. The length of the thread is equal to the required length of the foundation chain for the trim.
Using the yarn for the trim, make a foundation chain the length of the thread, turn.
<u>1</u>: 1 dc into 2nd ch from hook, 1 dc into every following ch.
Depending on the weight of your yarn, repeat row 1.
Crochet off.
Sew trim to jacket: see illustrations on page 32.

Grey pavement: Grey, turn at the end of each row.

The following instructions use the abbreviation ldc (long double crochet): Insert the hook around the long dc which was worked 2 rows below; the ldc are worked on the right side of the crochet piece.

1: 41 ch.

2: 1 dc into 2nd ch from hook, 39 dc [40 sts].

3: 1 ch, 3x (9 dc, 1 dc worked into row below [= into dc of row 2]), 10 dc [40 sts].

4: 1 ch, 40 dc.

5: 1 ch, 3x (9 dc, 1 ldc), 10 dc [40 sts].

6: 1 ch, 40 dc.

7: 1 ch, 3x (9 dc, 1 ldc), 10 dc [40 sts].

8: 1 ch, 40 dc.

9: 1 ch, 3x (9 dc, 1 ldc), 10 dc [40 sts].

10: 1 ch, 40 dc.

11: Work into bkl only; 1 ch, 3x (9 dc, 1 ldc), 10 dc [40 sts].

12: 1 ch, 40 dc.

13: 1 ch, 5 dc, 3x (1 dc worked into row below [= into dc of row 12], 9 dc), 1 dc worked into row below [= into dc of row 12]), 4 dc [40 sts].

14: 1 ch, 40 dc.

15: 1 ch, 5 dc, 3x (1 ldc, 9 dc), 1 ldc, 4 dc [40 sts].

16: 1 ch, 40 dc.

17: 1 ch, 5 dc, 3x (1 ldc, 9 dc), 1 ldc, 4 dc [40 sts].

18: 1 ch, 40 dc.

19: 1 ch, 5 dc, 3x (1 ldc, 9 dc), 1 ldc, 4 dc [40 sts].

20: 1 ch, 40 dc.

21: Work into bkl; 1 ch, 5 dc, 3x (1 ldc, 9 dc), 1 ldc, 4 dc [40 sts].

22: 1 ch, 40 dc.

23: 1 ch, 3x (9 dc, 1 dc worked into row below [= into dc of row 2]), 10 dc [40 sts].

24: 1 ch, 40 dc.

25: 1 ch, 3x (9 dc, 1 ldc), 10 dc [40 sts].

26: 1 ch, 40 dc.

27: 1 ch, 3x (9 dc, 1 ldc), 10 dc [40 sts].

28: 1 ch, 40 dc.

29: 1 ch, 3x (9 dc, 1 ldc), 10 dc [40 sts].

30: 1 ch, 40 dc.

31: 1 ch, 3x (9 dc, 1 ldc), 10 dc [40 sts].

Crochet off.

Florist's wire: Cut 2 pieces of wire. Calculate the length as follows: 2x leg length to below bust, the loop on the underside of the pavement.

Bend the wire: Make a figure eight, working from the centre. Bend the ends vertically upward. Poke both ends up in the desired spot through the pavement from underneath, spacing = space between the feet. Sew the pieces in place with stitches by hand, not exiting needle on right side. Measure a piece of wire for the outer edge (add an extra 8 cm /3¼ ins at start and end). Bend the wire into shape and lay along the outer edge on the underside of the pavement. Finish the outer edge with 1 rnd of dc, catching the florist's wire and working 1 dc into each dc and end of a row. Work 3 dc each into corners.
Insert the wire pieces through the heels up into the legs from underneath until the feet touch the pavement. Thread a needle with the thread in the colour of the shoes. Pass needle from below up on the front of the shoes and out. Insert needle back down again and knot thread on underside of pavement.

Pink handbag: see page 37.

CHIHUAHUA

CHIHUAHUA:

Head: Brown, close rnd with 1 sl st.
1: 6 dc into a thread ring
2: 1 ch, 6x inc 1 [12 sts].
3: 1 ch, 3x (3 dc, inc 1) [15 sts].
4: 1 ch, 15 dc.
5: 1 ch, 3 dc, 5x dec 1, 2 dc [10 sts].

6: 1 ch, dec 1, 5 dc into ftl,
    dec 1, 1 dc [8 sts], insert filling.
7: 1 ch, dec 1, 2 dc, dec 1.
Crochet off.
For the snout, pull the thread through the remaining 2 dc on rnd 6 and into the bkl of the dc on rnd 7, pull tight.

Eyes (2): Black.
Embroider 8 stitches to the right and left of the centre front 1 dc of rnd 5.
The eyes should protrude slightly.

Nose: Brown.
Exit needle in centre of snout. Embroider 4 stitches lengthwise over the middle.

Ears (each 2x): White for the inner ear, brown for the outer ear. Crochet 2 pieces for each ear:
1: 4 ch.
2: 1 dc into 2nd ch from hook, 2 dc [3 sts], turn.
3: 1 ch, 1 dc, dec 1 [2 sts], turn.
4: 1 ch, dec 1. Crochet off.

Lay inner ear on outer ear (inner ear lies on top), continue in brown.
From row 1, work 4 dc into side edge, 3 dc into the stitch at the top point,
4 dc into other side edge.
Sew on ears: Bend side edges slightly toward centre, sew to right and left of head over 3 stitches level with rnd 2.

Body: Brown, close rnd with 1 sl st.

1: 6 dc into a thread ring
2: 1 ch, 6x inc 1 [12 sts].
3: 1 ch, 3 dc, 3x inc 1, 6 dc [15 sts].
Change colour: colour for dog's coat (pink).
4: 1 ch, 4 dc, inc 1, 3 dc, inc 1, 4 dc,
    dec 1 [16 sts].
5: 1 ch, 14 dc, dec 1 [15 sts].

6: 1 ch, 5 dc, dec 1, 8 dc [14 sts].
7: 1 ch, 4 dc, dec 1, 8 dc [13 sts].
Change colour: brown (colour of body)
8: 1 ch, dec 1, 2 dc, dec 1, 3 dc, dec 1,
    2 dc [10 sts].
9: 1 ch, 2x dec 1, 6 dc [8 sts].
Crochet off, insert filling.
Pass thread through ftl of the remaining 8 dc, pull tight.

Sew head to body, with the belly facing down.

Tail: Brown.
1: 10 ch.
2: 1 sl st into 2nd ch from hook, 1 sl st, 7 dc.
Crochet off. Use the thread to sew on the ch of rnd 1 at the ftl of the dc of rnd 2.
Sew tail to top of body in centre back.

Legs (4): Brown.
1: 4 ch, close with 1 sl st.
2: 1 ch, 4 dc, 4 ch, 3 sl st into the 4-ch-foundation (1st sl st into 2nd ch from hook).
Crochet off. Attach legs: see page 36.

Attach Legs:

Cut 2 pieces of florist's wire (about 1.4 cm/ a good ½ in thick): 2x leg length + body width + 1 cm (⅜ in) (0.5 cm / ³/₁₆ inch will be bent at the ends).
Poke a piece of wire through the body from underneath where the front and back legs will be attached. Then pass the wire through the sl st on the leg to form the paw. Bend the wire end to a loop and poke back into the leg to conceal it from view.
Sew legs to body.
Attach the other 3 legs likewise.
Finally, bend the wire pieces exactly in the middle to allow the dog to stand.

Fur Trim for the Dog Coat
Work a length of chain with eyelash yarn or furry yarn at each transition from brown to pink (for the coat), work-ing very loosely and slightly elongating the stitches by pulling on them.

Neckband: Colour of your choice, I used black.

1: 12 ch.
2: 1 dc into 2nd ch from hook, 10 dc [11 sts].
3: 30 ch. Crochet off. Lay neckband around the neck, sew 1st and last dc together.

Handbag:

Colour of your choice, I used pink.
Begin with the handle.

1: 20 ch, 19 sl st into the foundation chain, working the 1st sl st into 2nd ch from hook.
2: 8 ch, 1 sl st into 1st ch of row 1.
    and close to a rnd, turn after every rnd from here.
3 to 6: 1 ch, 9 dc.
7: Work into bkl only; 1 ch, 9 dc.
8: 1 ch, 9 dc.
9: Work into bkl only; 1 ch, 9 dc.
10 to 13: 1 ch, 9 dc.

Button for the flap: white
1: 6 dc into a thread ring, close with 1 sl st.
2: 1 ch, 6 dc, close with 1 sl st.
Crochet off. Pass the thread through the ftl of the 6 sts, pull tight.
Sew button to front of flap.

14: Work into bkl only; 1 ch, 9 dc.
15: Join the bkl of the dc on rnd 14 and with the adjacent ftl of the dc on rnd 13: 1 ch, 9 dc.
16: no ch, work 1st dc into 2nd dc from hook, 5 dc, dec 1 [7 sts].
17: no ch, work 1st dc into 2nd dc from hook, 3 dc, dec 1 [5 sts].
18: no ch, work 1st dc into 2nd dc from hook, 1 dc, dec 1 [3 sts].
19: no ch, skip 1 dc, dec 1 (= crochet off 2nd and 3rd dc from hook together), 9 ch.
Crochet off.
Use this thread to close the 9-ch-foundation.
Close side edges of handbag.

SHALL WE DANCE?

LADY:

Crochet following the basic instructions on page 7.
Crochet the hair with Firenze colour 12 with sl st and lengths of chain. Then crochet the hair fringe. Sew the fringe to the top of the head.
Body, see p. 8, with wide skirt, see p. 9. Polka dots: see p. 18.
Straight legs: p. 14. Straight arms: p. 11.

GENTLEMAN:

Crochet head, ears, nose and eyes following the basic instructions on page 7.
Hair with Sicilia (Scheepjeswol): 2 ch between the sl st into 2nd ftl. Since this yarn is very thick, the dc can be omitted. Since the yarn has a fringed effect, lengths of chain are enough to cover the spaces between the sl st.

Shirt with Collar: Begin with white.

1: 6 dc into a thread ring, close with 1 sl st.
2: 1 ch, 6x inc 1 [12 sts] close with 1 sl st.
3: 1 ch, 6x (inc 1, 1 dc) [18 sts] close with 1 sl st.
4: 1 ch, inc 1, 3 dc, dec 1 [6 sts].
Work in rows back and forth from here, turn after each row.
5: 1 ch, 4 dc, dec 1 [5 sts].
6: 1 ch, 3 dc, dec 1 [4 sts].
7: 1 ch, 4 dc.
8: 1 ch, dec 1, 2 dc [3 sts].
9: 1 ch, 3 dc.
10: 1 ch, 1 dc, dec 1 [2 sts].
11: 1 ch, 2 dc.

12: 1 ch, dec 1 [1 sts].
13: 1 ch, 1 dc.
Crochet off.
Now continue with the colour for the collar.
1: 12 ch, now crochet into ftl of the 12 dc not worked on rnd 3 (of the shirt): 1 dc, 3x (inc 1, 2 dc), inc 1, 1 dc, 12 ch, turn.
2: 1 dc into 2nd ch from hook, 10 dc, work into ftl: 1 dc, inc 1, 5 dc, inc 1, 6 dc, inc 1, 1 dc; work into both loops of sts from here: 10 dc, dec 1 [41 sts], turn.
3: 1 ch, 1 dc into 2nd dc from hook, 37 dc, dec 1 [39 sts].
Crochet off.

39

Body: Begin with the colour for the trousers.

1: 6 dc into a thread ring, close with 1 sl st.

2: 1 ch, 6x inc 1 [12 sts].

Place CT marker, continue in spiral rnds.

3: 6x (inc 1, 1 dc) [18 sts].

4: 6x (2 dc, inc 1) [24 sts].

5: 1 dc, 5x (inc 1, 3 dc), inc 1, 2 dc [30 sts].

6: 6x (4 dc, inc 1) [36 sts].

7: 2 dc, 5x (inc 1, 5 dc), inc 1, 3 dc [42 sts].

8: 6x (inc 1, 6 dc) [48 sts].

9: 4 dc, 5x (inc 1, 7 dc), inc 1, 3 dc [54 sts].

10: 6x (inc 1, 8 dc) [60 sts].

11: 5 dc, 5x (inc 1, 9 dc), inc 1, 4 dc [66 sts].

Change colour: colour for the jacket

12: 4x (inc 1, 15 dc), 2 dc [70 sts].

13: Work into bkl only; 70 dc.

14 + 15: 70 dc.

16: 26 dc, 6x (dec 1, 1 dc), 26 dc [64 sts].

17: 20 dc, dec 1, 20 dc, dec 1, 20 dc [62 sts].

18: 16 dc, dec 1, 27 dc, dec 1, 15 dc [60 sts].

19: 10 dc, dec 1, 37 dc, dec 1, 9 dc [58 sts].

20: 3x (dec 1, 4 dc), 28 dc, 2x (dec 1, 4 dc) [53 sts].

21: 2 dc, dec 1, 8 dc, dec 1, 27 dc, dec 1, 8 dc, dec 1 [49 sts].

22: 6 dc, dec 1, 4 dc, dec 1, 23 dc, dec 1, 4 dc, dec 1, 4 dc [45 sts].

23: dec 1, 6 dc, dec 1, 27 dc, dec 1, 6 dc [42 sts].

24: 2 dc, dec 1, 5 dc, dec 1, 22 dc, dec 1, 5 dc, dec 1 [38 sts].

25: 3 dc, dec 1, 5 dc, dec 1, 16 dc, dec 1, 5 dc, dec 1, 1 dc [34 sts].

26: 2x dec 1, 30 dc [32 sts].

27: 7 dc, dec 1, 15 dc, dec 1, 6 dc [30 sts].

28: dec 1, 28 dc [29 sts].

29: dec 1, 27 dc [28 sts].

30: 28 dc.

31: 4 dc, 3x dec 1, 8 dc, 3x dec 1, 4 dc [22 sts].

32: 2 dc, 4x dec 1, 3 dc, 4x dec 1, 1 dc [14 sts].

33: 7x dec 1.

Crochet off. Pass the thread through the 7 ftl, pull tight. The stomach should later be in front.

Lay row 1 of the shirt on rnd 33 of the body, with the point of the shirt toward centre front of stomach (1st ftl of rnd 12 is visible). Sew the white point to the body, sew rnd 3 into bkl. Sew lengthwise edges of collar to white edge, collar ends meet in centre front.

For the lower part of the jacket, attach yarn to 1st ftl of rnd 12 and crochet into the 70 ftl of rnd 12, with the bottom of the body facing up.

1: 1 ch, 16 dc, dec 1 (into 2 ftl), 16 dc, dec 1, 16 dc, dec 1, 16 dc [67 sts], turn.

2: 1 ch, work 1st dc into 2nd dc from hook, 8x (6 dc, dec 1), inc 1 [59 sts].

Do not crochet off, but crochet a length of chain from centre of stomach to collar, with 1 dc into rnd 1 at lower jacket edge.

Buttons: 2 buttons in a colour of your choice:

1: 6 dc into a thread ring. Crochet off.

Sew buttons to right front.

Bow tie: Work in a colour of your choice, in rows back and forth. Turn at the end of each row.

1: 5 ch.

2: work 1st dc into 2nd ch from hook, 3 dc [4 sts].

<u>3</u> to <u>13</u>: 1 ch, 4 dc. Crochet off.
Join rnd 1 to rnd 13 to form a rind. Wrap the yarn around the middle about 10x to shape the bow tie.

Legs:

Crochet the legs as opposites, angled on the inside. This will ensure that the legs fit the body well. Begin with grey for the shoe.

<u>1</u>: 5 ch.

<u>2</u>: 3 dc into 2nd ch, 3 dc, contine on the other side of the 5-ch-foundation, 3 dc into 1st ch, 3 dc, close with 1 sl st [12 sts].

<u>3</u>: Work into bkl only; 1 ch, 4 dc, 4 tr crocheted off together, 4 dc [9 sts], close with 1 sl st.

<u>4</u>: 1 ch, 2 dc, 2x dec 1, 3 dc [7 sts], close with 1 sl st.

Change colour: Black for the trousers.

<u>5</u>: Work into bkl only; 5 dc, 2x inc 1 [9 sts]

Place CT marker, continue in spiral rnds.

<u>6</u> to <u>19</u>: See straight leg on p. 14.

Attach the legs following the instructions on page 15.

Arms (2x): Flesh colour, begin with hand:

1: 6 dc into a thread ring, close with 1 sl st.
2: 1 ch, 6 dc, close with 1 sl st.
3: 1 ch, 1 dc, 3 htr in 1, 2x dec 1 [6 sts], close with 1 sl st.
Change colour: Black for the sleeve.
4: Work into bkl only; 1 ch, 1 dc, inc 1, 2 dc, inc 1, 1 dc [8 sts]
Place CT marker, continue in spiral rnds.
If you crochet a cuff on the sleeve, work dc of rnd 4 into ftl only

5: 2 dc, inc 1, 5 dc [9 sts].
6: 3 dc, inc 1, 5 dc [10 sts].
7: 4 dc, inc 1, 5 dc [11 sts].
8: 4 dc, inc 1, 6 dc [12 sts].
9: 5 dc, inc 1, 6 dc [13 sts].
10: 5 dc, 2x inc 1, 4 dc, dec 1 [14 sts].
11: dec 1, 2 dc, inc 1, 2 dc, inc 1, 2 dc, inc 1, 3 dc [16 sts].
12: 2 dc, inc 1, 10 dc, inc 1, 2 dc [18 sts].
13 bis 18: 18 dc.
19: dec 1, 14 dc, dec 1 [16 sts].
20: dec 1, 12 dc, dec 1 [14 sts].
Insert filling and crochet off.

Cuff: White.

Attach thread to ftl of rnd 3, with hand in front.
1: 1 ch, 2x (2 dc, inc 1) [8 sts], close with 1 sl st.
2: 1 ch, 8 dc close with 1 sl st.
Crochet off.
When sewing the arm to the body, make a button in the colour of your choice on the outside of the cuff.

Carpet:

Crochet a rectangle. You can crochet the carpet in a plain colour or work stripes.
For the carpet, crochet 30 rows of 40 dc. Turn at the end of each row.
1: 41 ch.
2: 1 dc into 2nd ch, 39 dc [40 sts].
3 to 31: 40 dc.
Do not crochet off, but continue to crochet with light turquoise on the side edges at rows 31 to 2.
32: 3 dc into 1 st of row 31, 28 dc into ends of rows 30 to 3, 3 dc into 1 st of row 2, 40 dc into ch-foundation, 3 dc into 1 st of row 2, 28 dc into ends of rows 3 to 30, 3 dc into 1 st of row 31, 40 dc into dc of row 31.
33: Work the dc into the same points of insertion on rnd 32 (also around the dc of rnd 32), work dc into 1 st at corners: * 1 dc, 10 ch, 1 sl st into 1st ch of the 10-ch-length, 1 dc, rep from * until all 28 dc at the narrow sides have been worked, then work 40 dc along lengthwise edge, again at narrow edge rep from * to work the 28 dc, work 40 dc at 2nd lengthwise edge.
Crochet off.
Stabilise the legs with florist's wire to allow the couple to stand, following the instructions on page 33. Attach the points of the shoes to the carpet.

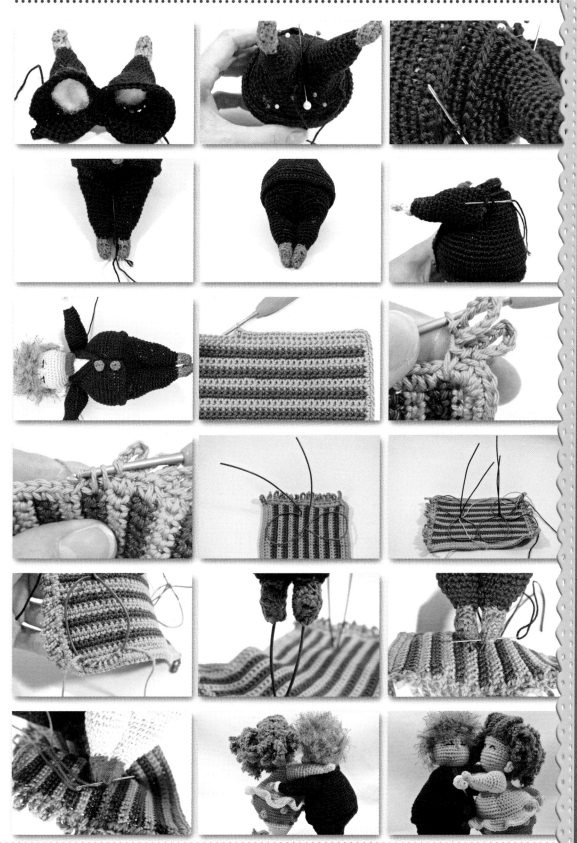

A DAY AT THE BEACH

FAT FABULOUS LADIES AT THE BEACH:

Crochet head, ears, nose and eyes: See basic instructions on page 7.
Arms for seated lady: straight arms on p. 11. Arms for lady lying down: bent arms, p. 11.
Hair: for seated lady of 100% wool 'Lopi' (Lettlopi), with lengths of ch and 1 sl st
in each front loop; for the lady lying down of Firenze colour 12 with sl st and lengths of ch.

Body with bathing suit or bikini:

Begin with the colour for the bathing
suit or bikini.
<u>1</u>: 6 dc into a thread ring, close with 1 sl st.
<u>2</u>: 1 ch, 6x inc 1 [12 sts].
Place CT marker, continue in spiral rnds.
<u>3</u>: 6x (inc 1, 1 dc) [18 sts].
<u>4</u>: 6x (2 dc, inc 1) [24 sts].
<u>5</u>: 1 dc, 5x (inc 1, 3 dc), inc 1, 2 dc [30 sts].
<u>6</u>: 6x (4 dc, inc 1) [36 sts].
<u>7</u>: 2 dc, 5x (inc 1, 5 dc), inc 1, 3 dc [42 sts].
<u>8</u>: 6x (inc 1, 6 dc) [48 sts].
<u>9</u>: 4 dc, 5x (inc 1, 7 dc), inc 1, 3 dc [54 sts].
<u>10</u>: 6x (inc 1, 8 dc) [60 sts].
<u>11</u>: 5 dc, 5x (inc 1, 9 dc), inc 1, 4 dc [66 sts].
<u>12</u>: 4x (inc 1, 15 dc), 2 dc [70 sts].
<u>13</u>: 2x (inc 1, 34 dc) [72 sts].
Bathing suit:
<u>14</u> to <u>17</u>: 72 dc.
<u>18</u>: 2x (2 dc, dec 1), 57 dc, dec 1, 2 dc, dec 1,
   1 dc [68 sts], continue on rnd 19.
Bikini:
<u>14</u> to <u>15</u>: 72 dc.
<u>16</u>: 71 dc, 1 sl st [72 sts].
Change colour: flesh colour.
<u>17</u>: Work into bkl only; 1 ch, 72 dc,
   close with 1 sl st.
<u>18</u>: 1 ch, 2x (2 dc, dec 1), 57 dc, dec 1,

2 dc, dec 1, 1 dc [68 sts]
Place CT marker, continue in spiral rnds.
<u>19</u>: dec 1, 11 dc, 3x (dec 1, 12 dc), dec 1,
   11 dc [63 sts].
<u>20</u>: 5 dc, 4x (dec 1, 11 dc), dec 1, 4 dc [58 sts].
<u>21</u>: 3x (dec 1, 4 dc), 22 dc, 3x (dec 1, 4 dc)
   [52 sts].
<u>22</u>: 3x (3 dc, dec 1), 22 dc, 3x (3 dc, dec 1)
   [46 sts].
<u>23</u>: 5x (dec 1, 6 dc), dec 1, 4 dc [40 sts].
<u>24</u>: 3 dc, 4x (dec 1, 6 dc), dec 1, 3 dc [35 sts].
<u>25</u>: 5x (dec 1, 5 dc) [30 sts].
<u>26</u>: 3 dc, 2x (dec 1, 8 dc), dec 1, 4 dc, 1 sl st
   [27 sts].
Bathing suit: Work into ftl only on rnd 27.
Bikini top: Change colour (= bikini top), close rnd
from here with 1 sl st.
<u>27</u>: 1 ch, inc 1, 26 dc [28 sts].
<u>28</u>: 28 dc. Change colour: flesh colour.
<u>29</u>: Work into bkl only; 1 ch, 28 dc.
<u>30</u>: 1 ch, 28 dc.
<u>31</u>: 1 ch, 5 dc, 3x dec 1, 8 dc, 3x dec 1, 3 dc
   [22 sts].
<u>32</u>: 1 ch, 2 dc, 4x dec 1, 3 dc, 4x dec 1, 1 dc
   [14 sts], insert filling.
<u>33</u>: 1 ch, 7x dec 1
Crochet off, stuff firmly with filling.

Legs: Both ladies have straight legs, see the basic instructions on p. 14.
<u>1</u> and <u>2</u>: in the colour of the shoes, then change colour: flesh colour.
<u>3</u> to <u>16</u>: see the basic instructions on p. 14.
Embroider 1 st across the foot in front for the strap (colour of your choice) (see illustration).
Sew on the legs.

Sunglasses:

Dark brown for the eyeglasses,
turn at the end of each row.

<u>1</u>: 5 ch
<u>2</u>: 1 dc into 2nd ch from hook, 3 dc [4 sts].
<u>3</u>: 1 ch, 4 dc.
Change colour: colour for the frame
<u>4</u>: 1 ch, work dc and sl st around the piece for the
   glass: 1 dc in each corner, work 3 sl st each clo-

se to edge between corners; begin with 1 dc
at corner, close rnd with 1 sl st into 1st dc.
<u>5</u>: <u>right</u> eyeglass: work 1 more sl st into the sl st
   of rnd 1, 14 ch, turn, work 13 sl st
   back into the 14 ch. Crochet off.
<u>5</u>: <u>left</u> eyeglass: work 2 more sl st into the sl st
   of rnd 1, 14 ch, turn, work 13 sl st back into
   the 14 ch. Crochet off.
Sew on the side pieces of the glasses with
1 stitch each.

Finishing the sunglasses:
Calculate the length of the florist´s wire: width across front of face (at eye level) + 2x the space front / ear + about 2 cm (¾ inch) for the loop at each end.
Cut 1 piece of wire of the calculated length.
Slip the wire through the back of the eyeglasses under the loops: first on the one side, then in the middle of the first eyeglass and then in the middle of the second eyeglass and finally through the other side piece.
Use the thread of the glasses frame to sew the wire to the glasses, also wrap the thread around the wire between the eyeglasses (the wire should be covered completely).

Attaching the eyeglasses:
Bend the end of the wire slightly and poke into the head behind the ear. Sew the side piece of the glasses in place on the head with the thread.
Bend the glasses into shape so that they sit centred on the face.
Attach the other side of the glasses at the other ear likewise.

Bathing suit: Embroider white polka dots on the bathing suit for the lady lying on the air mattress:

see page 18. Sew the legs to the underside of the body at rnd 1 exactly centred.
Note: The legs do not have to be sewn on the inside.

Iceream and Sun hat: Look at page 51.

AIR MATTRESS

AIR MATTRESS:

Striped Air Mattress:
Crochet the following 4 pieces:
– side piece in brown 2x
– back piece in brown 1x
– striped front 1x

Side piece (2x): Brown, turn at the end of each row.
<u>1</u>: 58 ch.
<u>2</u>: 1st dc into 2nd ch from hook, 56 dc [57 sts].
<u>3</u>+<u>4</u>: 1 ch, 57 dc.
Crochet off.

Back: Brown, turn at the end of each row.
<u>1</u>: 19 ch.
<u>2</u>: 1st dc into 2nd ch from hook, 17 dc [18 sts].
<u>3</u> to <u>64</u>: 1 ch, 18 dc, do not crochet off.
Continue to crochet at lengthwise edge of rows 64 to 2, also catching the side piece at the same time. For this, first insert hook into side piece and then into back. Begin at rows 2 to 4 of the side piece: First work 3 dc to corner of side piece and then along lengthwise edge:
<u>65</u>: 1 ch, 3 dc to corner of side piece, 57 dc to row 3 of back / corner of side piece, 3 dc into rows 4 to 2 of side piece and into rows 4 to 2 of back, 18 dc into row 1 of back, then catch 2nd side piece at other lengthwise edge, 3 dc into rows 2 to 4 of side piece and into rows 2 to 4 of back, 57 dc into back / corner of side piece, 3 dc into narrow edge of side piece and rows 62 to 64 of back, 18 dc into row 64 of back, close rnd with 1 sl st into 1st dc of rnd 65.
Crochet off.

Front: White and blue, stripe pattern: 2 rows in each colour alternately.
Begin with white, change colour after every odd numbered row except after row 1.
Turn after every row.

<u>1</u>: 19 ch.
<u>2</u>: Work 1st dc into 2nd ch from hook, 17 dc [18 sts].
<u>3</u> to <u>58</u>: 1 ch, 18 dc, do not crochet off.
<u>59</u>: Crochet round all edges in white, at the same time connecting upper edge of side piece/back by inserting hook into ftl (insert filling into mattress before completing rnd); turn at end of row 58 and connect with narrow edge of back: 1 ch inc 1, 16 dc, inc 1 into corner, 58 dc along lengthwise edge, inc 1 into corner, 16 dc in narrow edge, inc 1 in corner, 58 dc along lengthwise edge, close with 1 sl st into 1st dc.
Crochet off.

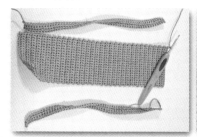  

<u>Finishing the air mattress:</u>
Use white thread and an embroidery needle to embroider a crosswise line to define the head section, inserting needle through mattress from the underside. Optional: Sew on 2 small buttons.

Sun hat: White, close rnd with 1 sl st.
<u>1</u>: 6 dc into a thread ring.
<u>2</u>: 1 ch, 6x inc 1 [12 sts].
<u>3</u>: 1 ch, 6x (inc 1, 1 dc) [18 sts].
<u>4</u>: 1 ch, 6x (2 dc, inc 1) [24 sts].
<u>5</u>: 1 ch, 3x (7 dc, inc 1) [27 sts].
<u>6</u>: 1 ch, 4 dc, 2x (inc 1, 8 dc), inc 1,
    4 dc [30 sts].
<u>7</u>: 1 ch, 3x (inc 1, 9 dc) [33 sts].
<u>8</u>: 1 ch, 5 dc, 2x (inc 1, 10 dc), inc 1,
    5 dc [36 sts].
<u>9</u>: 1 ch, 3x (inc 1, 11 dc) [39 sts].
<u>10</u>: 1 ch, 39 dc.
<u>11</u>: Work into ftl only; 1 ch, 1 dc,
    19x (inc 1, 1 dc) [58 sts].
<u>12</u>: 1 ch, 58x (1 dc, 3 ch), do not close rnd.
<u>13</u> to <u>17</u>: 58x (1 dc, 3 ch), always working dc around the ch-arch of the previous rnd, crochet in spiral rnds, close last rnd with 1 sl st.
Crochet off.

Ice cream cone:
Begin with light brown for the cone, close rnd with 1 sl st.

<u>1</u>: 3 dc into a thread ring.
<u>2</u>: 1 ch, inc 1, 1 dc, inc 1 [5 sts].
<u>3</u>: inc 1, 1 dc, inc 1, 1 dc, inc 1 [8 sts].
<u>4</u>: 1 dc, inc 1, 2 dc, inc 1, 3 dc [10 sts].
<u>5</u>: 3 dc, inc 1, 6 dc [11 sts].
<u>6</u>: 8 dc, inc 1, 2 dc [12 sts].
<u>7</u>: 3 dc, inc 1, 7 dc, inc 1 [14 sts].
Change colour: White. Work in spiral rnds from here into bkl
<u>8</u>: 7x (1 dc, inc 1) [21 sts].
<u>9</u>: 3x (4 dc, dec 1), 3 dc [18 sts].
<u>10</u>: 2 dc, 3x dec 1, 10 dc [15 sts].
<u>11</u>: 4 dc, 3x dec 1, 5 dc [12 sts].
<u>12</u>: 6 dc, 3x dec 1 [9 sts], insert filling.
<u>13</u>: 4x dec 1, 1 dc [5 sts].
<u>14</u>: dec 1, 1 dc, 1 ch.
Crochet off.

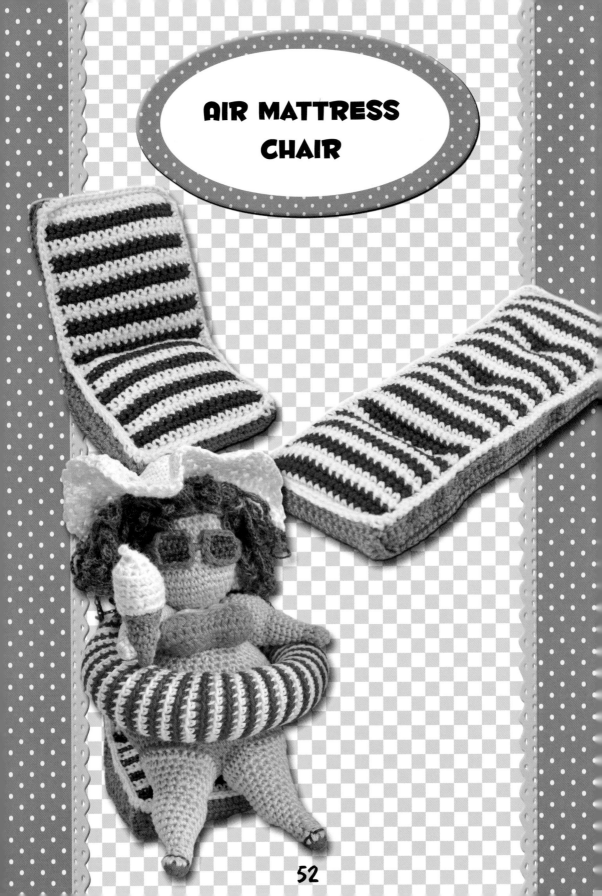

AIR MATTRESS CHAIR

AIR MATTRESS CHAIR:

Air mattress chair:
Crochet the following 4 pieces:
– side piece in brown 2x
– back piece in brown 1x
– striped front 1x

Side Piece (2x): Brown, turn at the end of each row.
1: 25 ch.
2: Work 1st dc into 2nd ch from hook, 23 dc [24 sts].
3: 1 ch, 23 dc, inc 1 [25 sts].
4: 1 ch, 25 dc.
5: 1 ch, work 1st dc into 2nd ch from hook, 2 dc, inc 1 [5 sts]
Work in short rows from here.
6: 1 ch, 3 dc, dec 1 [4 sts].
7 to 20: 1 ch, 4 dc. Crochet off.

Back: Brown, turn at the end of each row.
1: 19 ch.
2: Work 1st dc into 2nd ch from hook, 17 dc [18 sts].
3 to 51: 1 ch, 18 dc, do not crochet off.
Continue to crochet along lengthwise edge of rows 51 to 2, catching side piece at the same time.
Lay the side piece on the back to catch it in. Always insert the hook into the side piece first and
then into the back. Work a total of 51 dc, beginning with the 4 dc of row 20 on side piece:
Join the 4 dc of row 20 on side piece with the back.
52: 1 ch, 4 dc to corner of side piece and join with rows 51 to 48 on back, 19 dc to row 2 of side
piece, 24 dc into foundation chain of row 1 of side piece, 3 dc into rows 2 to 4 of side piece
and into rows 4 to 2 of back, 18 dc into row 1 of back, then continue along other lengthwise
edge and catch in the other side piece, 3 dc into rows 4 to 2 of the side piece and into rows
2 to 4 of the back, 24 dc into foundation chain of row 1 of the side piece, 19 dc to row 2 of side
piece, 4 dc into row 20 of side piece and into rows 48 to 51 of the back, 18 dc into row 51 of the
back, close rnd with 1 sl st into 1st dc of rnd 52.

Front: White and blue, stripe pattern: 2 rows in each colour alternately.
Begin with white, change colour after every odd numbered row except after row 1.
Turn after every row.

1: 19 ch.
2: Work 1st dc into 2nd ch from hook, 17 dc [18 sts].
3 to 38: 1 ch, 18 dc, do not crochet off.
39: Crochet round all edges in white, at the same time connecting upper edge of side piece/back
by inserting hook into ftl (insert filling into mattress before completing rnd); turn at end of
row 38 and connect with narrow edge of back: 1 ch inc 1, 16 dc, inc 1 in corner, 38 dc along
lengthwise edge, inc 1 in corner, 16 dc into narrow edge, inc 1 in corner, 38 dc along lengthwise
edge, close with 1 sl st into 1st dc.
Use white thread and an embroidery needle to embroider a crosswise line to define the sections of
the air mattress chair, inserting needle through mattress from the underside. Conceal thread.

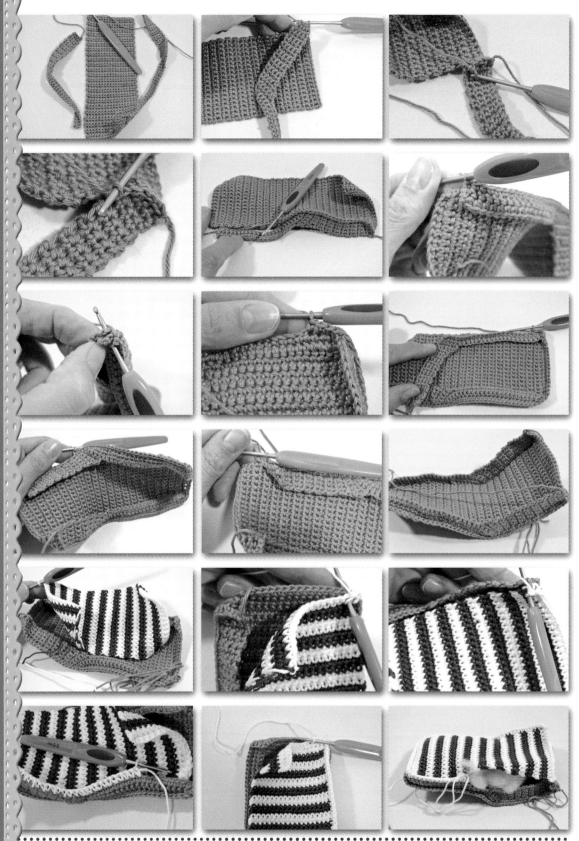

SWIM RING AND COCKTAIL

SWIM RING AND COCKTAIL

Swim Ring:

Two strands of yarn in 2 different colours are used to crochet the swim ring. Leave the yarn not in use hanging (do not crochet off!). Begin with white, colour A. Insert filling into the swim ring as you work.

<u>1</u>: 21 ch.

<u>2</u>: 1 dc into 2nd ch from hook, 19 dc [20 sts].

Leave colour A hanging.

Attach colour B <u>to 1st dc of rnd 2</u>.

<u>3</u>: 1 ch, 19 dc.

Leave colour B hanging.

<u>4</u>: colour A; begin working into 1st dc (= colour B) of rnd 3, to close the ring, 1 ch, 18 dc.

Leave colour A hanging.

<u>5</u>: colour B; 1 ch, 18 dc.

Continue in this manner and alternate colours until the ring is long enough (the swim ring should not be too tight around the waist).

I crocheted a total of <u>66</u> rnd.

It is necessary to end with colour B.

Then join the last rnd of the stuffed swim ring with the first white row, to close the shape to a ring.

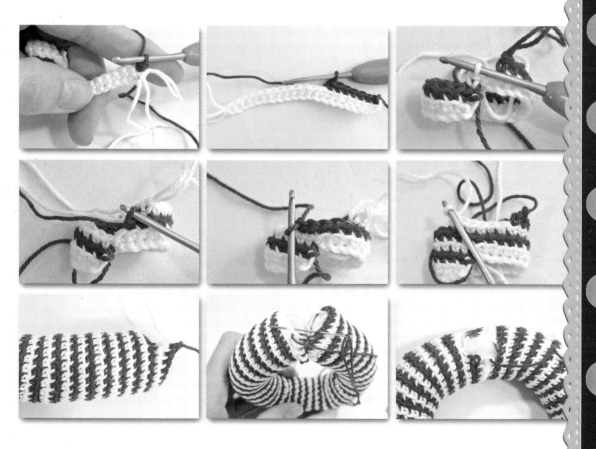

Cocktail:

Crochet a circle in red for the drink (this will be crocheted to the glass later).
<u>1</u>: 6 dc into a thread ring, close with 1 sl st.
<u>2</u>: 1 ch, 6x inc 1 [12 sts], close with 1 sl st.
Crochet off.

Base of glass: light grey; close rnd with 1 sl st.
<u>1</u>: 6 dc into a thread ring
<u>2</u>: 1 ch, 6x inc 1 [12 sts].
<u>3</u>: 1 ch, 6x (1 dc, inc 1) [18 sts].
Cut a piece of florist's wire (about 1.4 cm/ a good ½ in thick) the desired length: circumference
base of glass + 3x length of drinking straw (e.g. from base of glass to upper edge of drinking straw).
Bend wire in the middle to form a circle (circumference of base = rnd 3), twist ends together once
and then stand them up vertically.
<u>4</u>: Work into bkl only; 1 ch, 6x (dec 1, 1 dc) [12 sts], lay the circle of wire inside the base of the glass
   between rnds 3 and 4 before closing the rnd. Work your stitches around the wire from here.
<u>5</u>: 1 ch, 6x dec 1 [6 sts].
<u>6</u>: 1 ch, 2x (1 dc, dec 1) [4 sts].
<u>7</u>: 1 ch, 4 dc.
Change colour: red for the drink.
<u>8</u>: Work into ftl only: 1 ch, 4x inc 1 [8 sts].
<u>9</u>: 1 ch, 8x inc 1 [16 sts].
<u>10</u>: 1 ch, 4x (inc 1, 3 dc) [20 sts].
<u>11</u>: 1 ch, 20 dc.
<u>12</u>: 1 ch, 4x (dec 1, 3 dc) [16 sts].
<u>13</u>: 1 ch, 4x (dec 1, 2 dc) [12 sts].
Change colour: grey for the glass.
Poke the wire ends through the red circle where desired. Lay circle
on upper edge of red piece and connect to rnd 13 with the next rnd, always first inserting
needle into dc of rnd 13 and then into ftl of the dc of the circle.
Note: Insert filling into glass before closing the rnd.
<u>14</u>: 1 ch, 12 dc.
<u>15</u>: 1 ch, 4x (inc 1, 2 dc) [16 sts].
Crochet off.

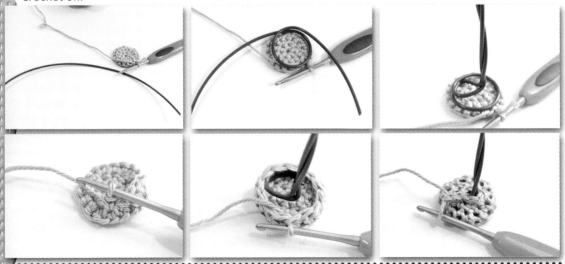

For each drinking straw, make a lengths of chain with pink and with yellow (slightly longer than the wire), turn, crochet back with dc, working 1st 1 dc into 2nd ch from hook, crochet off. Lay the strip around the wire and close the lengthwise edges with needle and thread.

Fruit: orange.

1: 6 dc into a thread ring, close with 1 sl st.
2: 1 ch, 3x (inc 1, 1 dc) [9 sts], close with 1 sl st.
3: 1 ch, 3x (dec 1, 1 dc) [6 sts], close with 1 sl st.
Crochet off. Pass the thread through the 6 ftl, place the fruit over the end of the yellow straw, pull thread tight and conceal.

FAT FABULOUS BALLERINAS

FAT FABULOUS BALLERINAS

Crochet following the basic instructions on page 7. The skirt will be crocheted otherwise.
Both ladies have straight arms, see p. 11.
See page 62 for the legs.
Sew the ballerinas' hands together in this pose to allow them to stand.
Hair: 100% new wool 'Lopi' (Lettlopi), use 1 strand of yarn, no lengths of ch.

Body:

Begin with colour for panties.

1 to 13: see basic instructions.
Crochet a wide skirt: see p. 8.
14: 71 dc, 1 sl st [72 sts].
If the upper body is to be a different colour
than the panties, change colour now.
15: Work into bkl only; 1 ch, 72 dc.
Place CT marker, continue in spiral rnds.
16 + 17: 72 dc.
Set piece aside.

Ballet skirt:
Attach white yarn for the ballet skirt to ftl
of a dc on rnd 14, rnd 17 faces you, the bottom
lies underneath.
1: 36x (1 dc, inc 1) [108 sts].
Place CT marker, continue in spiral rnds.

2: 54x (1 dc, inc 1) [162 sts].
3: 81x (1 dc, inc 1) [243 sts].
4: 22x (inc 1, 10 dc), 1 dc [265 sts].
Crochet off now for the shorter skirt
(pink ballerina).
Continue as follows for the longer skirt
(blue ballerina):
5: 6 dc, 21x (inc 1, 11 dc), inc 1, 6 dc
   [287 sts].
6: 22x (inc 1, 12 dc), 1 dc [309 sts].
Crochet off.

Continue with the body, see basic instructions
on page 9: body with narrow skirt
18 to 33.
Crochet off.

Cut a piece of florist's wire (about 1.4 cm/ a good ½ in thick) the desired length: 2x arm + 1x
diameter of upper body (at arm level).
Poke wire through upper body at arm level and bend ends each to a loop so that they are no
 longer sharp. Slip arms onto wire at right and left. Insert filling into arms.
Check placement of arms by pinning them before sewing them to sides of body, almost flattening
rnd 18. The arms should be a bit moveable. Then sew arms in place.
Position the pink ballerina in a split with arms bent up.
The blue ballerina is on tip toe with arms bent forward to hold on to the other ballerina.

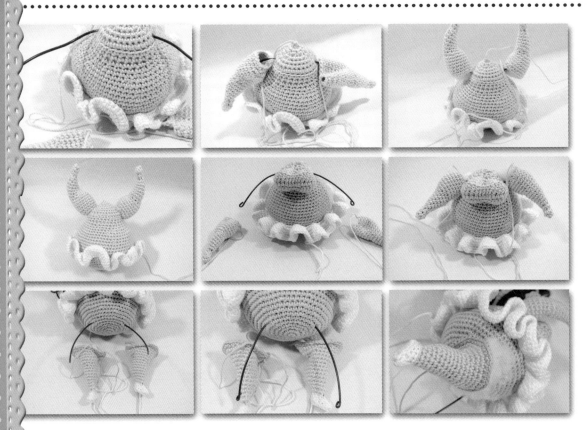

Head band for blue ballerina:

<u>1</u>: 35 ch.

<u>2</u>: 1 dc into 2nd ch from hook, 33 dc [34 sts], turn.

<u>3</u>: 1 ch, 34 dc.

Crochet off. Sew ends together in centre back, lay band around head and sew in place.

Legs: Begin with white for the ballet slippers.

<u>Blue ballerina:</u> Crochet straight legs, see basic instructions on page 14.

Use florist's wire to give the legs stability as for the arms. Cut a piece of wire the desired length. Poke wire through body to fit the legs, then slip wire ends into legs, bend loops at wire ends. Insert filling into legs and sew to body. Join inside of legs together.

<u>Pink </u>ballerina: Crochet legs as follows:

<u>1</u>: 5 ch.

<u>2</u>: 3 dc in die 2. ch, 3 dc, continue on the other side of the 5 ch-foundation, 3 dc into 1st ch, 3 dc, close with 1 sl st [12 sts].

<u>3</u>: Work into bkl only; 1 ch, 4 dc, 4 tr crocheted off together, 4 dc [9 sts], close with 1 sl st.

Change colour: flesh colour.

<u>4</u>: Work into bkl only; 1 ch, 2 dc, 2x dec 1, 3 dc, work 1 more dc (into 1st dc of rnd 4).

Place CT marker, continue in spiral rnds.

<u>5</u>: 5 dc, 2x inc 1 [9 sts].

<u>6</u>: 7 dc, 2x inc 1 [11 sts].

<u>7</u>: 8 dc, 2x inc 1, 1 dc [13 sts].

<u>8</u>: 7 dc, inc 1, 4 dc, inc 1 [15 sts].

<u>9</u>: 11 dc, inc 1, 3 dc [16 sts].

<u>10</u> + <u>11</u>: 16 dc.

<u>12</u>: 12 dc, dec 1, 2 dc [15 sts].

<u>13</u>: 4 dc, inc 1, 1 dc, inc 1, 8 dc [17 sts].

<u>14</u>: 6 dc, inc 1, 10 dc [18 sts].

<u>15</u>: 14 dc, Work into ftl only: 4x inc 1 [22 sts].

<u>16</u>: 2 dc, inc 1, 8 dc, inc 1, 4 dc, inc 1, 2 dc, inc 1, 2 dc [26 sts].

Work underlined sl st into ftl.

<u>17</u>: 2 dc, inc 1, 2 dc, <u>6 sl st</u>, 2 dc, inc 1, 4 dc, inc 1, 4 dc, inc 1, 2 dc [30 sts].

18: inc 1, 3 dc, 2 sl st, 6 sl st into sl st of rnd 17, 2 sl st, 3 dc, inc 1, 4 dc, inc 1, 2 dc, inc 1, 3 dc, 1 sl st [34 sts].
Change colour: colour for panties.

19: 1 ch, 3 dc, 2 sl sl, 10 sl st into previous sl st, 2 sl st, 4x (3 dc, inc 1), 1 dc close with 1 sl st. Crochet off.

Tie slippers around legs with a white thread: Begin in centre back, bring thread forward, cross in front, bring thread back, sew in place at 1 dc, bring forward and then to centre back again. Conceal end of thread.

Finally, sew the hands of the ballerinas together as illustrated.

Have fun being creative!

Anja Toonen

Dutch: www.haakpret.nl
German: www.haekelfreude.de

Translation: Linda Tsardakas;Layout: Karine Müller